T3-BPX-766

Reprints of Economic Classics

THE

INFLUENCE AND DEVELOPMENT

OF

ENGLISH GILDS

THE
INFLUENCE AND DEVELOPMENT

OF

ENGLISH GILDS

AS ILLUSTRATED BY THE HISTORY OF
THE CRAFT GILDS OF SHREWSBURY

BY

FRANCIS AIDAN HIBBERT

[1891]

REPRINTS OF ECONOMIC CLASSICS

AUGUSTUS M. KELLEY · PUBLISHERS
NEW YORK 1970

First Edition 1891

(Cambridge: At The University Press, 1891)

Reprinted 1970 by

AUGUSTUS M. KELLEY · PUBLISHERS

REPRINTS OF ECONOMIC CLASSICS

New York New York 10001

. . . .

S B N 678 00630 X

L C N 79 107907

. . . .

PRINTED IN THE UNITED STATES OF AMERICA
by SENTRY PRESS, NEW YORK, N. Y. 10019

THE

INFLUENCE AND DEVELOPMENT

OF

ENGLISH GILDS.

𝕮𝖆𝖒𝖇𝖗𝖎𝖉𝖌𝖊 𝕳𝖎𝖘𝖙𝖔𝖗𝖎𝖈𝖆𝖑 𝕰𝖘𝖘𝖆𝖞𝖘. 𝕹𝖔. V.

THE

INFLUENCE AND DEVELOPMENT

OF

ENGLISH GILDS:

AS ILLUSTRATED BY THE HISTORY OF
THE CRAFT GILDS OF SHREWSBURY.

BY

FRANCIS AIDAN HIBBERT, B.A.,

OF ST JOHN'S COLLEGE, CAMBRIDGE; ASSISTANT MASTER IN DENSTONE COLLEGE.

THIRLWALL DISSERTATION, 1891.

𝕮𝖆𝖒𝖇𝖗𝖎𝖉𝖌𝖊:
AT THE UNIVERSITY PRESS.
1891

PREFACE.

I SHOULD explain that, in the present Essay, I have restricted myself to associations which had for their object the regulation of trade. Frith Gilds and Religious or Social Gilds have received only passing notice.

The Merchant Gild is too wide a subject to be treated in an Essay such as this. Moreover the records of the Shrewsbury Merchant Gild are too meagre to afford much information, and I would therefore have gladly passed over the whole question in silence but that without some notice of it the Essay would have seemed incomplete.

My attention has thus been concentrated on the Craft Gilds, and on the later companies which arose out of these.

It is greatly to be regretted that we have no work on Gilds which deals with the subject from an English point of view, and traces the development of these pre-eminently English institutions according to its progress on English soil.

The value of Dr Brentano's extremely able Essay

is very largely diminished, for Englishmen, not only
because he is continually attempting to trace undue
analogies between the Gilds and Trades Unions, but
still more because he has failed to appreciate the
spirit which animated English Merchants and Craftsmen in their relations with one another, and so has
missed the line of Gild development in England.   If
he had not confined his attention, so far as English
Gilds are concerned, solely to the London Companies
he could hardly have failed to discover his mistake.

Something has been done to set the facts of the
case in a clearer light by Dr Cunningham briefly in
his *Growth of English Industry and Commerce*[1].

But it is to be feared that Mr J. R. Green's
History is so deservedly popular, and Mr George
Howell's *Conflicts of Capital and Labour* is so
otherwise reliable, that views differing from those
which these writers set forward—following Dr Brentano as it appears—stand little chance of being
generally known.

Great as is the weight which must attach to such
important authorities, I have endeavoured—by looking at the facts in my materials from an independent
standpoint—to avoid being unduly influenced by
their conclusions, or by a desire to find analogies
where none exist.

The materials from which I have worked call for
but little description.   They are simply the records
of the Shrewsbury Gilds—either in their original
form as preserved in the town Museum and Library,

---

[1] I speak of the old edition. I have not had the advantage of
using the newer work.

or as printed in the Shropshire Archæological Society's *Transactions*.

Though my view has been thus confined it has been kept purposely so. English local history is its own best interpreter, and although in some instances the documents have required illustrating and supplementing from extraneous sources, these occasions have been few. At the same time I have not omitted to notice how the effects of national events were felt in provincial changes, and I have especially striven to point out how the Shrewsbury records bear upon the various theories which have been put forward respecting Gilds. Writing thus in a historical rather than an antiquarian spirit I have not considered it necessary to overburden the pages with needless footnotes referring repeatedly simply to the records of the Shrewsbury Gilds.

October, 1890.

NOTE.—*The Gild Merchant*, by Charles Gross, Ph.D. (Oxford, Clarendon Press, 1890), appeared after the above had been written and the Essay sent in. I have since had the advantage of reading it. The general conclusions at which the writer arrives are so similar to those I had already formed, that I have not found it necessary to alter what I had written. I have however to some extent made use of the material he has brought together in Vol. II., chiefly by way of strengthening the authorities in the footnotes to which reference is made in the text.

EXTRACT FROM THE REGULATIONS FOR THE THIRLWALL PRIZE.

"There shall be established in the University a prize, called the 'Thirlwall Prize,' to be awarded for dissertations involving original historical research."

"The prize shall be open to members of the University who, at the time when their dissertations are sent in, have been admitted to a degree, and are of not more than four years' standing from admission to their first degree."

"Those dissertations which the adjudicators declare to be deserving of publication shall be published by the University singly or in combination, in an uniform series, at the expense of the fund, under such conditions as the Syndics of the University Press shall from time to time determine."

CONTENTS.

NOTE.

On page 26 Liverpool should be inserted. The charter was granted in 1229, by the king.

CHAPTER I.

INTRODUCTORY.

In these days of convenience and easy transit, *Local* when distance has been annihilated by the telegraph *life in England* wire and the express train, we can hardly realise, *always* even with an effort, the extent to which such changes *varied.* have revolutionised the social life of Englishmen. Of local sentiment there can be now but little, yet local sentiment has played a greater part in our history than perhaps any other motive. The England of to-day is little more than a great suburb of its capital. Yet it is a peculiar feature of the England of the past that its local life was always singularly varied, not only in the Middle Ages but down to quite recent times. Indeed the characteristic is still more than traceable in some of our less busy districts.

In the past, too, some parts possessed the feature in a more marked degree than others. We should naturally expect that few towns would have a stronger infusion of local feeling than Shrewsbury. Through all its history it has indeed been marked by strong individuality.

*Early
growth of
Shrews-
bury.*

Situated in the midst of the Marches of Wales, the centre round which long waged the struggle for the fair lands westward of the Severn, its strong walls and insular position soon gave it a marked commercial superiority over the surrounding country. In consequence we find Shrewsbury at an early date considerably more advanced than the unprotected land outside, which lay open to the ravages of the Welsh. This condition of affairs, the reverse of favourable for commercial advancement, continued to depress the neighbourhood after Edward the First's conquest of the Principality, for the disorders of the Lords Marchers kept the Borders in a state of continual alarm, and prevented the inhabitants from settling down to any regular and profitable industry[1].

Henry IV. on the death of Glendower effected the reconquest of Wales, and enacted severe laws against the inhabitants. The only result was, however, the organisation of robber bands whose definite object was to plunder and harass more completely their English neighbours. The evil became so intolerable that a special court had to be erected to remove it, and in 1478 was formed the Court of the President and Marches of Wales.

By dint of powers of summary jurisdiction over disturbers of the public peace, a diminution was

---

[1] That the land did not contain a population adequate for its cultivation is evident from a Statute of 1350 which allows the people of the Marches of Wales (and Scotland) to go about in search of work at harvest-time, as they had been accustomed to do aforetime. (*Rot. Parl.* II. 234.) *Work and Wages*, pp. 131—2.

effected in the disorders, and the border lands were
able to participate in the increase of trade which was
such a marked feature of the fourteenth century.
In spite of the temporary shock given to industry by
the Reformation, the district had, by the latter part
of the sixteenth century and the beginning of the
seventeenth, quite recovered from the Welsh ravages,
and its prosperity at this time was very remarkable.

The fertility of the district brought wealth to the
market towns, and provided a wide area of comfortable purchasers for the products of their industries. The expansion of the Welsh cloth trade
gave rise to a twofold struggle. There was firstly
a strenuous effort of the border towns to keep it to
themselves, and secondly a private quarrel as to
which of them should engross the market. Shrewsbury eventually secured the monopoly after an
arduous contest, and the importance of the town
was thus considerably enhanced.

The internal history of its Gilds will show how *Its later*
peculiarly the state of Shrewsbury illustrates the *prosperity.*
period of quiet prosperity before the introduction of
machinery broke in upon the comfortable life of
provincial England.

The county towns then possessed an importance
of which they have since been shorn by various
causes[1]. Each was the capital of its district, filling
the part of a distant metropolis to which neither the
country gentleman nor the wealthy burgess could

---

[1] Cf. Thackeray, *The Four Georges*, p. 320, "decayed provincial
capitals, out of which the great wen of London has sucked all
the life."

expect to go more than once or twice in a lifetime. Shrewsbury, in particular, was possessed of features which serve not only to make it especially typical of the social habits of the period, but which at the same time give it an interest exceptionally its own[1].

*Its sta-
tionary
condition
in recent
times.*

And when the introduction of machinery transformed the face of England to such a large extent, the changes which it brought to Shrewsbury were extremely slight. Local life was strong. The town was slow to accommodate itself to new conditions of industry. Its Gilds and companies maintained their vigour to the end. Their yearly pageant continued to our own day. The timbered houses which the substantial tradesmen built in the days of their prosperity are still, many of them, standing. The streets of the town have been only gradually altered and improved. They still follow the old lines, often inconvenient, but always interesting: they still are called by their old names, full of confusion to the stranger, full of significance to the student.

*Import-
ance of
history of
its Gilds.*

*Their
quiet de-
velopment.*

Shrewsbury, then, exhibits a character eminently its own, from whatever point we view its history. But it is a distinction of similarity rather than the prominence of singularity. The progress of the town has gone on quietly and calmly, seldom interrupted and never forced. The history of its Gilds must of necessity present similar features. It will be a record of silent development, often leaving few traces, yet not the less evident to careful observation.

[1] Macaulay. *History of Eng.*, Vol. i. pp. 165—6. Infra, Chap. vii.

But it is also a history in studying which we must be particularly on our guard against being led astray by the analogy of similar institutions in other parts of England or on the Continent. The desire to arrive at, or to conform to, general conclusions often blinds writers to the fact to which we have already drawn attention, namely, that local life in England was always varied; that each town and district had its own strongly-marked peculiarities. Bearing this in mind, deviations—apparent or real—from the ordinary course of Gild history will cause us no surprise. The shearmen's maypole quarrel[1] with the bailiffs is almost the only trace of serious conflict at Shrewsbury between the municipal authorities[2] and the companies until the seventeenth century. There are no signs of the rise of Yeomen Gilds[3] in earlier or later years, though evidence in plenty is found of the complete disregard shown by the masters for the interests of the journeymen[4]. On the other hand, so far from the Court of Assistants being a late creation we meet with it at Shrewsbury very early in Gild history. *Peculiarities.*

It will also be a record rich in illustrations of contemporary social life[5]. The closeness of relationship between religion and the ordinary business pursuits of the mediæval burgess; the wide public *Especial points of value.*

---

[1] Cf. infra, Chap. vii.

[2] Brentano, 44, 52, 54, 58. Green, *Short Hist.*, 193. G. Howell, *Conflicts of Capital and Labour*, 22—25, 29, 31.

[3] Cunningham, *Growth of Industry*, 212. Brentano, 90, 95.

[4] Cf. infra, Chap. v.

[5] Cf. especially Chap. vii.

influence exercised by the Gilds in their earlier years, and the remarkable family feeling they maintained within the boundaries of the old towns even down to the time when the companies had become utterly demoralised, will be exemplified not less remarkably than the continuity of the Gild sentiment through the shocks of the Reformation period, through the economic changes of Elizabeth, and even (in some sort) through the Reforms of 1835.

It is a history too which will help us to understand a problem of considerable difficulty. We shall not only see the degenerated societies of capitalists in full vigour down to the date of their enforced termination as trading companies, but we shall also be enabled to perceive how it was that they managed to retain their prejudicial and antiquated privileges to the very end of their existence.

It is indeed in the light which their history throws on the conditions of provincial trade and the social customs of an ordinary provincial town during the seventeenth and eighteenth centuries that its special importance lies. The rapid progress which marked the commencement of that period, not less than the torpor and decay which characterised the corporate towns at its close will be found to be eminently exemplified in the history of the Shrewsbury Gilds.

CHAPTER II.

THE MERCHANT GILD.

DR BRENTANO[1] is particularly desirous to make *Univer-* it clear that he considers England " the birthplace of *sality of* Gilds." But it is scarcely necessary to point out *feeling.* that the conception of the Gild belongs to no particular age and to no particular country. Not to insist unduly on the universality of an institution from which some writers have derived the Gilds, and to which they certainly bear considerable resemblance, the family—common to humanity itself —we note that the Greeks had their ἔρανοι[2] and their ξυνωμοσίαι[3], and the Romans their *collegia opificum*[4], each exhibiting not a few of the features

---

[1] *The Hist. and Development of Gilds.* Cf. especially Note 1.

[2] *Ibid.* 8. " The objects of the ἔρανοι were of the most varied description ;...associations of this kind were very common in the democratic states of Greece, and to this class the numberless political and religious societies, corporations, unions for commerce and shipping, belonged." Boeckh, *Public Economy of Athens,* p. 243.

[3] Grote, *Hist. of Greece*, Vol. VI. p. 247, n. 1, where several interesting parallels with the Mediæval Gilds will be found. (Cf. also infra, p. 34, note 2.)

[4] E. Hatch, Bampton Lectures, Lect. II. notes.

of the mediæval Gilds. *Corps des métiers* existed in France in very early times, perhaps in direct continuation of the Roman institutions, and played a great part in the beginnings of many towns[1]. So early as to be anterior to the earliest known Frith Gilds, that is to say in the latter half of the seventh century, a regularly organised system of confederation existed among the Anglo-Saxon monasteries throughout England, according to the rules of which the united Abbeys and Religious Houses undertook to pray for the members, living and departed, of one another[2].

Each of these associations, so various in date and object, bore great resemblance to the Gilds of later times, according as the latter are considered in the light of some one or other of their functions : now it is the common feast, now it is the possession of corporate property, here it is the union of all the workmen of a craft into one sodality, there it is the association of neighbours for mutual responsibility and protection ; now it is the confraternity "in omni

---

[1] Cunningham, p. 124.

[2] Cf. *Die klösterlichen Gebets Verbrüderungen bis zum Ausgange des Karolingischen Zeitalters,* von Dr Adalbert Ebner. Similar spiritual confederations are found in Italy in the second quarter of the eighth century, and in the ninth they become common in southern Europe. Alcuin speaks of them by the terms *pacta caritatis, fraternitas, familiaritas.* The monks of the allied houses were termed *familiares.* Dr Brentano (p. 20) says that at later times "conventions like that between the Fraternity of London Saddlers and the neighbouring Canons of St Martin-le-Grand, by which the saddlers were admitted into brotherhood and partnership of masses, orisons, and other good deeds with the canons, were common."

obsequio religionis." Such a tendency to association is simply the result of man's gregarious nature, and there is no need to restrict what is found alike in all peoples and all periods. But it is none the less true that the tendency has been more strongly marked in England than elsewhere. The earliest Gild Statutes which have come down to us are English[1], and the development of Gilds in England *English and Continental Gilds.* proceeded according to its normal course without being diverted and confused by external and disturbing circumstances. The real history of Gilds will thus be the history of *English* Gilds, not of those of the Continent, whose records detail rather a bitter struggle between rival classes in the towns[2]. If the constitutional importance of the Gilds was thus greater on the Continent than it was in England[3], this was because *there* a social institution was dragged out of its proper sphere of action, and in the arena of politics was shorn of the most attractive of its features.

In these pages we shall be concerned solely with examples drawn from the history of our own country. Where necessary reference will be made to the institutions of other towns, but in general our attention will be concentrated on one provincial borough only—a town, as we have seen, well calculated to illustrate the social life of England in

[1] Brentano, pages 1, 2. They are printed in Kemble's *The Saxons in England*, Vol. I. Appendix D.

[2] Brentano, 49.

[3] Gneist, *Self Government*, Vol. I. p. 110; *Verwaltungsrecht*, Vol. I. p. 139.

Value of history of local Gilds. the past. It is only by working out the several departments of local municipal history that anything like a complete view of the subject can be ultimately obtained[1]. In the following chapters an attempt will be made to contribute something towards such a consummation.

The records of the later Craft Gilds at Shrewsbury are entirely satisfactory, but unfortunately those of the Merchant Gild are of the most meagre description. They throw but little light therefore on its functions or history, and still less on the interesting question as to the precise nature of the relationship which existed between the Gilda Mercatória and the Communa. Our attention will consequently be chiefly directed to an examination of the history and development of the *Craft Gilds*. A few remarks, more or less general in their scope, on the Merchant Gild seem however to be called for, in anticipation of the history of the later trade associations.

Growth of towns in twelfth century. In England, as elsewhere, the growth of the towns was one of the most marked features of the twelfth century. This was due to various causes. William's conquest had opened up increased facilities for communication with the Continent: the Norman soldiers brought skilled Norman traders in their train, and so war ministered to commerce just as subsequently the Crusades were largely helpful to the growth of trade and the progress of the towns. The vigorous adminstration of Henry I. and Henry II. had also facilitated the expansion

[1] Stubbs, iii. 576, 578.

of industry. Henry I. favoured the rising towns both because of their commercial utility and in order to make use of their counterbalancing influence against the power of the Barons. Shrewsbury he took into his own hands, having enforced the surrender of the town from the rebellious Robert de Belesme. The amendment of the currency and the organisation of the Courts of King's Bench and Exchequer were also as favourable to material prosperity as were the legal reforms of Henry II. afterwards. The circuits of the Justices Itinerant were restored, and appeals to the king in Council were established. A further weakening of baronial power was also effected by the destruction of the castles which the lawlessness of Stephen's tenure of the sovereignty had permitted; while the introduction of scutage made the king in some measure independent of the feudal forces by enabling him to call in the support of mercenary troops. On the other hand the Assize of Arms restored the national militia to its old important place.

Shrewsbury had seemed to be depressed by the conquest. The town had been granted, in the first instance, to Roger de Montgomery, whose two great works, his castle and his abbey, yet remain. Both the earl and his works were at first the cause of complaint. In Domesday Book it is pointed out that Montgomery had destroyed 51 houses to make room for his castle: to the abbey he had granted 39 burgesses; 43 houses in the town were held by Normans and exempted from taxation. Consequently, as the same sum was required from the town as had been paid *tempore regis Edwardi,* the burden fell with undue hardship on the English inhabitants who remained.

But the ultimate result of both castle and monastery was beneficial to the town. The latter attracted trade and the former protected it[1], and Shrewsbury early became a commercial centre of some importance.

They differed little from country, The towns at this period differed but little from the country. They both engaged in agriculture as well as trade; they were alike governed by a royal officer, or by some lord's steward. In the towns the houses were of course more closely clustered, and a further difference arose afterwards in the fact that a freeman in the town, when admitted to the Gild, *except in possession of a Merchant Gild* might be landless[2]. The chief distinction indeed between town and country lay in the fact that the former had a Merchant Gild.

The origin of such commercial unions is lost in the dimness of antiquity. Even in Anglo-Saxon times Dover had its Gildhall, and Canterbury and London are said to have been also possessed of trading associations. They came into being at first *to preserve peace.* probably to preserve peace. At the date of the Conquest the right of jurisdiction almost invariably belonged to whoever held the town, but we cannot conceive that Roger Montgomery's successors would be likely to concern themselves overmuch with internal police. As a fact it would rest with the

[1] *Work and Wages,* p. 126.
[2] Stubbs, I. 452.

burghers themselves to protect their goods and
persons from mishap.

Frith Gilds, with much the same objects, had *A.-S.Frith*
been common anterior to the Conquest[1]. In most *Gilds.*
places where there was a market it was essential
that some recognised authority should be in existence to keep the peace, as well as to be witness to
sales[2]. The "laws of the city of London" were
apparently drawn up with the express design of
supplementing defective law[3]. They exhibit to us
a complete authority for the supervision of trade,
corresponding to the later Merchant Gild in nearly
every particular : there is the common stock, the head
man, the periodical meetings at which "byt-fylling"
plays its usual important part[4]. The "ordinance
which King Ethelred and his Witan ordained as 'frith-
bot' for the whole nation" imposed the duty of pur-
suing offenders on the town to which they belonged[5].
There was thus evidently some organisation within
the boundaries of the town, and as the chief of the
burgesses forming this organisation were also the
chief merchants (since trade was the *raison-d'être* of
the towns) it soon began naturally to frame commercial regulations[6]. So the Town Gild became, *Trade*
when, after the Norman Conquest, trade had as- *regula-*
sumed important dimensions, the Gilda Mercatoria *tions.*

[1] Stubbs, I. 449 : *Select Charters*, 63, cap. 27, 28 : 67, cap.
iii., viii., 1., etc.

[2] *Select Charters*, 66, 12 : 72, 6.

[3] Stubbs, I. 450.

[4] *Select Charters*, 67, iii., viii., 1.

[5] *Ibid.* 72, ii. cap. 6.

[6] Cunningham, 129, Stubbs, I. 452, Brentano, 42.

Royal authori- sation: earliest mention. with exclusive powers and privileges by royal charter. The earliest unmistakable mention of a Merchant Gild is at the end of the eleventh or the beginning of the twelfth century[1]. Under Henry I. grants of Merchant Gilds appear in one or two of the charters granted to towns[2], and under Henry II., Richard and John they become more frequent[3]. Shrewsbury was one of the few which had the Merchant Gild confirmed as early as the reign of Henry II.[4]

By these charters what had originally been a voluntary association now became an exclusive body to which trade was restricted.

Important as were the advantages gained by the procuring of such royal authorisation, these charters only set the seal to what had existed in effect before. The landed and mercantile interests were practically identical within the towns: the great merchants were also the great landowners; the Gilda Mercatoria could thus frame regulations which it would be extremely difficult for any trader to disregard[5].

Functions. Besides, the benefits which resulted from common trading would be too obvious for any individual who could procure entrance into the Gild to abstain from doing so. It was far more to the common interest that one representative should buy for all and then divide the purchase equitably than that each should

[1] Gross, I. 5 ; II. 28, 37. See note 1 to this Chapter.
[2] Cf. note 1 to this Chapter.
[3] *Ibid.*
[4] *Select Charters*, 167 etc. ; Stubbs, I. 452, and n. 1 ; Eyton's *Shropshire*, XI. 134.
[5] *Quarterly Review*, Vol. 159.

compete with each and so minister simply to the profit of the seller.

There are several examples of such combined purchasing by a royal or municipal officer in towns where there was no Merchant Gild[1]. It was however generally effected by means of the latter, the granting of which meant the according of permission to the members to settle for themselves their custom in buying and selling.

The retail trade within the town was restricted to their own members individually, and the wholesale trade coming *to* the town was reserved to themselves collectively. Members of the Merchant Gild alone might sell within the walls, and traders coming from without might sell only to the Merchant Gild.

There was no danger then as there would be now of such a practice driving all trade away from the town, for the restrictions in force at one place would be paralleled almost exactly in every other. At the periodical fairs alone did free trade prevail.

But the exclusive privileges might be exceedingly harmful if the main body of householders were not members of the Merchant Gild. It was then the fact that the restricted trading was not " to the advantage of the community of the borough but only to the advantage of those who are of the said society[2]." When however the great majority of the householders were members of the trading corporation the arrangement would work well and beneficially for the whole town.

[1] Gross, I. 135, 136 and notes; II. 133, 149.   [2] *Ibid.* I. 42.

*All Bur-
gesses are
Gildsmen.*

The effect of the granting of royal authorisation was, therefore, to finally draw all burgesses into the Gild, for all townsmen of any importance were traders. The records of the Shrewsbury Merchant Gild, though of the scantiest description, are sufficient to show how comprehensive was its range. All branches of trade were, at least down to the time of Edward I., represented in it[1]; it comprised every rank and degree, proportioning its fines and payments accordingly. The progress of the fusion of races is shown by the lists of names, which are both Saxon and Norman in indiscriminate order.

So closely indeed did the practical boundaries of Gild and town coincide that in many places the former seemed to become the Communa, when the kings began to grant charters of incorporation. Richard I. can even say that all the privileges of his charter are granted " *civibus nostris Wintoniæ de gilda mercatorum*[2]," seeming to imply that at Winchester at least there were no citizens extraneous to the Merchant Gild. The villain flying from his lord could only be admitted to freedom through the machinery of the Merchant Gild. The Merchant Gild was ready to the hand of the burgesses as a centre, and the only centre, round which to rally when engaged in defending their liberties or in procuring fresh privileges. On the other hand the existence of such a secure and wealthy body, which would be at all times able to ensure payment of

---

[1] Cf. note 2 to this Chapter.
[2] *Select Charters*, 265.

the *firma burgi*, and the frequent royal assessments which were laid upon the towns, would be an additional inducement to the kings in granting the charters of liberties. Glanvill, in the time of Henry II., doubtless already looked on the Merchant Gild and the Communa as, for all practical purposes, identical[1], from which the inference seems to lie that the possession of such a gild had thus early come to be looked upon as the sign and symbol of municipal independence. It is true that a town *might* become a free borough without possessing a Merchant Gild, but this would be an exception to the general rule. It would be similar to the case of a free borough not holding the *firma burgi:* such a contingency was possible but unusual. To the mind of the lawyer therefore the possession of a Merchant Gild seemed the necessary precursor of a royal charter of privileges. And in practice this was found to be, speaking generally, the case.

Duties of Gildsmen.

Tendency to amalgamation of Gild and Communa.

This apparent identity of Burgesses and Gildsmen would find palpable expression in the fact of the Gild Hall becoming the Town Hall. This naturally did not take place to any considerable extent before the 14th century, though during that period it became fairly common. It may have been that the Merchant Gild permitted the use of its Hall for public purposes, at first only occasionally and then more and more frequently until at length what had been exceptional became normal (either through precedent or purchase[2]); certain it is that

[1] *Select Charters*, 162, "Communam scilicet gildam."
[2] Gross, I. 83 and note 1.

the two names of Gild Hall and Town Hall became
practically synonymous in about the 14th and 15th
centuries. This had been foreshadowed at an early
date. Domesday Book spoke of the "gihalla Burgensium[1]" at Dover.

At Shrewsbury, in a charter of 1445, the Town
Hall is called, as it is at this day, the Gildhall.

*But all
Gildsmen
not
Burgesses.*
But the *ideas* of Gild-members and townsmen
were long kept separate. Burgess-ship depended on
residence[2] and the possession of a burgage-tenement,
but not so membership of the Merchant Gild, which
often comprised among its numbers many outsiders[3]. In this way the two bodies were clearly
distinguished. At Ipswich it was ordered in John's
charter[4] that the statutes of the town were to be
kept distinct from those of the Gild "as is elsewhere
used in cities and boroughs where there is a Gild
Merchant," for the latter would probably consist of
both "de hominibus civitatis" and also "de aliis
mercatoribus comitatus[5]." Ecclesiastics[6] and women
might also be members of the Gild, but of course
could not be burgesses. Such members had, in some
towns, to pay additional fees[7].

The charters were always granted to the "Bur-

---

[1] Stubbs, i. 451.

[2] *Select Charters* (Helston), 314.

[3] Gross, i. 54. The Rolls of the Shrewsbury Merchant Gild
contain a large number of names of "foreigners." For instance
in 1209 there were apparently 56 foreigners; in 1252 these had
increased to 234.

[4] Printed in Gross, ii. 114—123.

[5] *Select Charters*, 166 (Charter of Henry II. to Lincoln).

[6] Gross, ii. 235, and cf. note 2 to this Chapter.

[7] Cf. the "Chepgauel" at Totnes. Gross, ii. 236.

gesses," without reference to their capacity as Gild-members, except in the cases where the privileges granted were such as would only concern members of the Gild. It was the "burgesses" who purchased the *firma burgi* and who paid such goodly sums for trading and other privileges. But in making up these payments they were glad to avail themselves of the assistance of the non-burgess merchants, not the least of whose recommendations seemed doubtless to lie in the share they were willing to bear in contributing to the periodical tallages and similar royal charges. They were indeed as a document expresses it most serviceable when it was requisite "*defectus burgi adimplere*[1]." Although in name it was the burgesses who paid the money and who purchased the *firma burgi*, it was in fact the Merchant Gild which bore the largest part.

Distinction between Gild and Communa preserved in Charters,

but not in practice.

In another way also the "foreigners" who were members of the Merchant Gild were useful to the burgess-members of it.

During earlier years all the Craftsmen who so desired, and could afford the necessary payments, were admitted into the Gild of Merchants. The designation 'merchant' was then extended to all who engaged in trade. But as the Gilda Mercatoria became in practice more and more identical with the Communa the idea seems to have grown up that landless men, renters of their shops within the towns, should not be admitted to the Gild.

For in this period, that is during the 14th and 15th centuries, the old democratic government of

Gild seems to become Communa.

---

[1] Gross, I. 57.

the towns was giving place to a close governing council[1]. This was in no sense the Merchant Gild, though probably all the members of the select body would be members of the Gild[2]. Being also the most important of its members they would be able to use its influence for their own ends, and in these measures they would generally have on their side the majority of the "foreigners," who would not know or care much about the internal concerns of the town. Thus it came about that having secured important trading privileges the influence of the Merchant Gild was chiefly directed, though by a small coterie of its members, towards municipal rather than mercantile objects.

Rise of Craft Gilds

These latter it left to be dealt with by the new companies into which the craftsmen were beginning to amalgamate. In this action they were helped and encouraged by the Merchant Gild, or as it now

favoured by Merchant Gild and Communa.

was in practice, the municipal authority. It is a mistake to speak of the rise of the Craft Gilds in England as a movement bitterly hostile to the Merchant Gilds and therefore strenuously opposed by the latter. The reverse was the fact. The increased complexity of the task of regulating trade,

This favour natural

as division of labour developed and commerce expanded its bounds, became difficult, and the central

---

[1] Owen and Blakeway, i. 169—174. Erskine May, *Const. Hist.* iii. 276—77.

[2] This close relationship of, and actual difference between, the two bodies is very distinctly seen at Bristol in the reign of Edward IV., when it was the custom for the Mayor and Council of the town to choose the chief officers of the Merchant Gild, and to pass ordinances for its regulation. Gross, ii. 25.

body was for this additional reason glad to depute *under the* its powers to, and to exercise its functions through, *circumstances* smaller and specialised agencies. The charters of *and proved* the Craft Gilds too contain no articles which would *by the Charters.* stand the members in stead in a conflict with a higher power, whereas if these charters had been the hardly-won prize of a severely contested struggle they would assuredly have contained some bitter articles in consequence of the past and in preparation for the future. We shall however examine the rise and history of the Craft Gilds in the subsequent chapters.

The substance of the foregoing paragraphs may *Summary.* be briefly summarised thus.

The most noticeable feature in the Economic history of England during the years immediately succeeding the Norman Conquest was the growth of the towns. They differed however but little from the country districts in government except in the particular that they possessed a Merchant Gild.

These trading corporations are first unmistakeably perceived soon after the Conquest, originating probably in the need which arose, as the towns increased in wealth and importance, for the existence of some authority to preserve peace within their borders, as without peace and order trade could not prosper.

Such an union for securing internal peace, consisting as it did of the principal persons interested, easily went on to enact commercial regulations. These were, on the one hand, the reserving to its own body the privilege of purchasing the stock of the foreign merchant, and, on the other, restricting the right of selling within the town to its own members. Royal authorisation set the seal to this practice. When the kings began to give charters to the towns, the legal recognition of their Merchant Gild was one of the chief of the privileges desired by the townsmen.

This restricted trading was not prejudicial to the town because practically all the burgesses were members of the Gild. If they all were not Gildsmen *before* the royal authorisation they would be likely to become so afterwards.

But all Gildsmen were not burgesses. The latter *must* be residents: the former frequently included outsiders among their number.

Nevertheless as the years went by, the Gild seemed to become the Communa, even as the Gild Hall became the Town Hall. Various reasons conduced to this. There were practically no burgesses extraneous to the Merchant Gild, though there were often Gildsmen who were not burgesses. The Merchant Gild was the only machinery for freeing the fugitive villain after a year and a day's residence in the town. It also afforded the best, and as a fact the only, centre round which the burgesses could rally in the defence of their old privileges or in the struggle for fresh ones. Its wealth and stability were also an additional inducement to the kings in granting to the towns their *firma burgi*. In theory the Gilda Mercatoria might be kept distinct from the Communa, but in practice the two bodies were found to be identical. But the later Communa did not take cognisance of trade affairs except indirectly through the Craft Gilds which the increasing complexity of trade was calling into being. Many of the members of these latter bodies were members of the Merchant Gild, and to them were added large numbers of the lesser craftsmen. The Craft Gilds specialized the work of the Merchant Gild, which gradually ceased to discharge any important office as a collective whole, though through the many branches into which it had ramified its influence continued to be of the greatest importance to the welfare of town and trade.

NOTE 1.

THE following is an attempt to construct a table of grants of the Merchant Gild (down to 1485), in chronological order, and showing also, where possible, by whom the grant was made.

Unfortunately the list is in several cases only approximately correct, as the document from which I have obtained my date shows that the Merchant Gild has evidently been granted at some previous time. In all cases however the earliest known mention of the Gild is given.

In compiling this table I should acknowledge my plentiful use of the materials recently made available in *The Gild Merchant*, by Charles Gross (Oxford, 1890).

William II. and Henry I. (1087–1135)

Burford 1087–1107	Earl of Gloucester
Canterbury 1093–1109	

Henry I. (1100–35)

Wilton 1100–35	King
Leicester 1107–18	Robert, Earl of Mellent
Beverley 1119–35	Abp Thurstan of York
York 1130–31	

Stephen (1135–54)

Chichester	King
Lewes	Reginald de Warrenne

Stephen and Henry II. (1135–89)

Petersfield

Henry II. (1154–89)

Carlisle	King
Durham	
Fordwich	
Lincoln	King
Oxford	
Shrewsbury	King
Southampton	King
Wallingford	King
Winchester	King
Marlborough 1163	King
Andover 1175-6	King
Salisbury 1176	King
Bristol 1188	John, Earl of Moreton

Richard I. (1189–99)

Bath 1189	King
Bedford	King
Gloucester	
Nottingham	John, Earl of Moreton
Bury S. Edmund's 1198	

John (1199–1216)

Chester 1190–1211	Earl of Chester
Dunwich 1200	King
Ipswich 1200	King
Cambridge 1201	King
Helston 1201	King
Derby 1204	King
Lynn Regis 1204	King
Malmesbury 1205–22	
Yarmouth 1208	King
Hereford 1215	King
Bodmin 1216	King
Totnes 1216	King
Newcastle-on-Tyne 1216	King

Henry III. (1216–1272)

Preston
Haverfordwest

Portsmouth
Worcester 1226–27   King
Bridgenorth 1227   King
Rochester 1227   King
Montgomery 1227   King
Hartlepool 1230   Bp of Durham
Dunheved (Launceston) 1231–72   Richard, Earl of Cornwall
Newcastle-under-Lyme 1235   King
Liskeard 1239–40   Richard, Earl of Cornwall
Wigan 1246   King
Sunderland 1247   King
Cardigan 1249   King
Reading 1253   King
Scarborough 1253   King
Guildford 1256
Kingston-on-Thames 1256   King
Boston ? 1260
Macclesfield 1261   King
Coventry 1267–68   King
Lostwithiel 1269

Edward I. (1272–1307)

Berwick
Bridgwater
Congleton   Henry de Lacy
Devizes   King
Welshpool   Griffith, Lord of Cyveiliog
Aberystwith 1277   King
Windsor 1277   King
Builth 1278   King
Rhuddlan 1278   King
Lyme Regis 1284   King
Caernarvon 1284   King
Conway 1284   King
Criccieth 1284   King
Flint 1284   King
Harlech 1284   King
Altrincham 1290   Hamon de Massy
Caerswys 1290   King
Overton 1291–2
Newport (Salop) 1292

Chesterfield 1294	John Wake
Kirkham 1295	King
Beaumaris 1296	King
Henley-on-Thames 1300	? Earl of Cornwall
Barnstaple 1302	
Newborough 1303	King

Edward II. (1307–1327)

Llanfyllin	
Ruyton 1308–9	Earl of Arundel
Wycombe 1316	
Bala 1324	King

Edward III. (1327–1377)

Gainsborough	Earl of Pembroke
Bamborough 1332	
Grampound 1332	
Lampeter 1332	
Denbigh 1333	King
Lancaster 1337	
Cardiff 1341	Hugh le Despenser
Nevin 1343–76	Prince of Wales
Llantrissaint 1346	Hugh le Despenser
Hedon 1348	King
Hope 1351	Prince of Wales
Pwllheli 1355	Prince of Wales
Neath 1359	Edward le Despenser
Kenfig 1360	Edward le Despenser
Newton (S. Wales) 1363	Prince of Wales

Richard II. (1377–1399)

Axbridge	
Newport 1385	Earl of Stafford
Oswestry 1398	King

Henry IV. (1399–1413)

| Saffron-Walden | |
| Cirencester 1403 | King |

Henry V. (1413–1422)

None

Henry VI. (1422–1461)

Plymouth 1440
Walsall 1440
Weymouth 1442
Woodstock 1453   King

Edward IV. (1461–1483)

Ludlow 1461   King
Grantham 1462
Stamford 1462
Doncaster 1467
Wenlock 1468

Richard III. (1483–1485)

Pontefract

NOTE 2.

LIST OF TRADES, HANDICRAFTS AND PROFESSIONS COM-
PRISED IN THE LISTS OF MEMBERS OF THE SHREWS-
BURY MERCHANT GILD.

apotecarius, specer, spicer—
apothecary
aurifaber—goldsmith
baker, bakere, pistor, pictor—
baker
barber, tonsor, tyncer—barber
bercarius, tannator, tanner—
tanner
botman—corn-dealer
brewer—brewer
carnifex—butcher
carpentarius, faber—carpenter
carrere—carrier
cementarius—? plasterer
cissor, tailur, taylor, tayleur,

parmentarius, parminter,
parmonter—tailor
clericus—clerk
cocus—cook
colier, coleyer—collier[1]
comber—? wool-comber
corvisarius, gorwicer, corde-
waner, sutor—shoemaker
coupere, hoppere (?)—cooper
deyer—dyer
forber—sword-cutler
ganter, cirotecarius, glover—
glover
garnusur—garnisher
grom—groom

[1] On the early use of coal, cf. *Work and Wages*, p. 124.

gunir, gynur—
harpour—harper
haukerus, hawkerus, hawker—
 hawker
justice—judge
leche—leech
loxmith, locker, lok—locksmith
mason—mason
mercer—mercer, merchant or
 retailer of small wares
molendarius—miller
palmer—
pannarius—draper, clothier
petler, ? pelterer—seller of skins

piscator—fisherman
potter—potter
prest, presbyter—priest
sadeler—saddler
scriptor—transcriber
sherer, shearman—clothworker
tabernarius, taverner—tavern-
 keeper
teynterer—
walker or waller—? builder
webbe—weaver
wodemon—woodman
wolbyer—wool-buyer

CHAPTER III.

THE CRAFT GILDS.

The Merchant Gild   WE have seen how the Merchant Gild consisted of all the traders whose business lay in the town. Such an association, though nominally open to all whether landowners or not who could afford to pay the requisite fees, was in essence oligarchical, and this feature became in course of time its most apparent characteristic. We saw, also, how there grew up a large class extraneous to the privileged *and the craftsmen.* Merchant Gild. This body of outsiders became continually larger and more important. The Welsh ravages in the exposed country would induce numbers to seek the friendly shelter of the town, which by this continuous infusion of fresh blood, found its trade become more and more flourishing, and consequently its attractions to "foreigners" more and more powerful. Each branch of industry was also incessantly receiving large accessions of strength in the shape of fugitive villains from the country-side, who, by residence during a year and a day were released from fear of a reclaim to serfdom. These new settlers, some of whom the advance of time found making considerable strides towards prosperity, seeing themselves shut out from the Town Gild both by the exclusive spirit of that body and by the fact that they themselves were not owners of land within the town[1], but (even in the case of the wealthiest of them) only renters of their shops, were naturally drawn, by the spirit of the times, towards amalgamation[2].

It was natural that men working at the same trade,—living probably in the same neighbourhood[3], and during intervals of rest exchanging gossip from adjacent door-steps,—meeting one another in all the actions of daily life and with thoughts and language running in similar grooves,—should also desire to be not separated in worship. Likewise, in time of trouble, when death brought gloom to the house of a fellow-workman, or when through accident or misfortune he failed to appear at his accustomed place in yard or workshop, it was by the ordinary promptings of nature that his brother craftsmen came to offer their sympathy and help. And so we find the men of the various trades forming themselves into fraternities, in order to pour united supplications for Divine assistance and to offer thanks in common for Divine favour[4]. The Tailors

Tendencies to union among the latter:

Religious,

[1] The Statutes of Labourers first gave a recognised position to the "men who neither held land, nor were free burgesses," but who had a dwelling, and paid the rates of some town. Cf. Cunningham, 193—4. Supra, p. 19.

[2] *Quarterly Review*, Vol. 159; *Economic Interpretation*, p. 298.

[3] Cf. "Butchers' Row" at Shrewsbury, where also the High Street was formerly called Bakers' Row (Pidgeon's *Handbook*, old Ed. p. 37). The Street which was afterwards known as Single Butcher Row had been earlier called "Shoemakers' Row" (Phillips, p. 200).

[4] Cf. the Monks' Gilds alluded to above, p. 8 and n. 2.

and Shoemakers had their chantries in St Chad's
Church, where the Weavers also had their especial
altar, maintaining in addition a light before the
shrine of St Winifred in the Abbey of the Holy
Cross. The Drapers of the town early became
drawn together in a religious brotherhood, the chapel of which in the collegiate church of Our Lady
was the object of frequent and solicitous care when
the fraternity of the Holy Trinity was definitively
changed into the Worshipful Company of the Drapers.
In the church of St Juliana the altar of the Shearmen stood in the north aisle, where a chaplain said
their special mass for a yearly stipend of £4[1].

It was the pride of the Gilds to expend the best
efforts of their wealth and skill on the embellishment
and maintenance of their chapel, upon which they
were able to look as their own. Their worldly possessions at no one time reached a figure high enough
for them to provide a large endowment for church or
chantry, but the thankofferings of the years sufficed
for all current expenses. The fixed stipend was
small, but the fabric, raised and adorned as funds
allowed, was commodious and beautiful[2].

It was to this ever-present desire to consecrate
some portion of the yearly profits of trade to the

[1] " Which is now the only fragment left to the incumbent of the
Church's income before the Reformation." S. A. S. x. 223.
[2] Longfellow expresses this well in *The Golden Legend:*
" The Architect
" Built his great heart into these sculptured stones,
" And with him toiled his children, *and their lives*
" *Were builded, with his own, into the walls,*
" *As offerings unto God.*"

honour of Him who had given the increase, that the annual pageant owed its pomp. The Corpus Christi procession was an occasion of especial prominence at Shrewsbury, where the Gild charters and records are full of minute regulations for its order.

The associations of fellow workmen for the pur- *Social,* poses of religion also took the form of clubs for mutual benefit and assistance. The Drapers were maintaining their school and schoolmaster in 1492[1]; their almshouses were only rivalled by those of the Mercers. The maintenance of poor and decayed members was always one of the most prominent of the objects of association. Attendance at the last offices by the grave of a deceased brother, and remembrance of him in prayer, were likewise universal duties of brethren. Edward VI.'s confiscation of Gild property broke down in all the towns a great system of poor-relief which had hitherto freed the government of that most difficult problem. Nor did the Gilds wait until a brother was completely crushed before they came to his assistance. Fluctuations of trade then as now sometimes brought occasions of temporary embarrassment. But "the false and abominable contract of Usury...which the more subtily to deceive the people they call 'exchange' or 'chevisance,' whereas it might more truly be called 'mescheaunce,'" ...was rightly looked upon as unworthy of fellow-workers for the common good, " seeing

---

[1] At Worcester a Gild School educated 100 scholars. The substitute which the Government provided at the Reformation was for less than half that number. Toulmin Smith's Collection, p. 203 and note.

that it ruins the honour and soul of the agent, and sweeps away the goods and property of him who appears to be accommodated, and destroys all manner of right and lawful traffick[1]." The common chest of the Gild was therefore at the service of the brethren[2], not, as in the days of degeneracy, to aid the capitalist in grinding down his workmen, but to keep the craftsman from the clutches of the usurer.

Com-mercial.

Out of these religious fraternities and social clubs developed what we may more correctly term Craft Gilds; or to speak more strictly we should perhaps rather say that many of these societies began to add to their social and religious objects an additional one, namely trade regulation[3]. They would be encouraged in this direction by the action of the Merchant Gild, or its successor the municipal authority, which, as the expansion of trade necessitated specialisation, was glad to depute its powers to such associations[4].

Early Craft Gilds.

The earliest mention of Craft Gilds is in the reign of Henry I., when notice is found of the Weavers of London, Oxford, Winchester, Lincoln and Huntingdon, the Cordwainers of Oxford and the Fullers of Winchester[5]. They became more common and more

---

[1] Ordinances of the City of London, framed in 1363.

[2] The Greeks had private Societies called θίασοι and ὀργεῶνες which also presented this feature.   Cf. Foucart, *Les Associations réligieuses chez les Grecs.*

[3] Brentano, 54.   Cunningham, 203, n. 2.

[4] Cf. supra, p. 20.   In writing thus I have not forgotten that an opposite view is taken by Dr Brentano, Mr J. R. Green, Mr Geo. Howell, and in fact most of the writers who have touched on the subject.

[5] Gross, I. 114.

influential as the development of industry was fostered by the central government. This was especially the policy of Edward I. and Edward III. By the end of the 14th century the Craft Gilds become numerous. As they took over the duties and functions *Effect of* of the Merchant Gild the existence of the latter *their growth on* was rendered to a considerable extent superfluous, *Merchant Gild.* and the merging of the Gilda Mercatoria into the Communa became not only inevitable but convenient and natural. During the 14th and 15th centuries, when the Craft Gilds attained their highest power, the decay of the Merchant Gilds became very marked.

In some places where this happened the name of *The later* the Merchant Gild wholly disappeared. In others *"Merchant* where the expression continued in use the institution *Gild."* changed its character and became simply a religious fraternity. In a few instances the select corporation alone inherited the name : in some the whole body of freemen did so. Again, there are examples of a survival of the expression as applied to the whole body of tradesmen, that is the whole of the members of the various Gilds[1]. A Patent of Queen Elizabeth, dated 1586, thus alludes to the aggregate of unions under the collective name of " the Gild of Burgesses of Shrewsbury." In the same way we read of " the several companies belonging to the guild merchant of Reading," "the Guild of Merchants in Andever, which Guild is divided into three several Fellowships," etc.

---

[1] Hartlepool, 1673. " It is ordered at a general guild...that whosoever...shall presume to come in and within the liberty of this corporation, to trade or occupye...to the prejudice of the free trades and companyes within the corporation " etc. Gross, II. 106—7.

Just as the Merchant Gild differentiated itself into Craft Gilds, the Craft Gilds afterwards again in the aggregate took the name and style of the Merchant Gild.

If such additional proof were needed this action on their part might be adduced in support of the assertion, which cannot be too strongly emphasised or too often repeated, that in England there was no conflict between the Merchant Gild and the Craft Gilds. Though these latter associations had grown up in vindication, as it might seem, of the principle of free amalgamation in opposition to oligarchical exclusiveness, and although it was evident that as they *Identity of* increased the Merchant Gild must decline, yet there *interests of* was at no time any idea of antagonism between the *Corpora-* two kinds of authority within the town. On the *tion and* contrary internal police was very materially assisted *Gilds* by the Gilds[1]. They carried on the good work which *seen in* the Merchant Gild had inaugurated. Not only were *Police* dissensions among combrethren to be brought before *regula-* the Wardens and Stewards instead of forming the *tions;* occasion of unseemly brawls and disturbances, but one of the objects for which the associations existed is expressly stated to be "for the weale, rest and tranquilitie of the same towne, and for good rule to be kept there[2]." With this object in view the composition of the Tailors and Skinners (1478) contains several articles which show how materially the officers of the Gild assisted the bailiffs of the town[3].

[1] Cunningham, 209, n. 1.

[2] Tailors' Composition, of 1478.

[3] The Bailiffs are to apprehend on the third day any person coming to the town "suspitiouslie w^{th}oute anie lawfull errand

The Gild officers, though freely elected by the *evidenced* combrethren took their oaths of office before the *by supervision of* bailiffs of the town, who also secured, if necessary, *municipal* the enforcement of the ordinances of the Gilds[1]. *authorities,* The town authorities exercised, too, a general supervision: it seems to have been the rule for the compositions to be annually (or periodically) inspected; and for new regulations to be subject to municipal approval[2].

One consequence of this authorisation by the *(therefore* town officials was that the latter ceased to take *supported by them;)*

or occasion," and to detain him in prison " till he have found suertie of his good bearing or els to avoide the towne." "And if anie man be comitted to their warde by the wardens wth the fower men ordeigned to the said wardens to be assistaunt in counsell in good counsell giving of anie crafte wthin the said Towne and Fraruncheses that then that person that is so comitted to warde...be not deliv'ed out of warde by the Bailiffs wthout assent and agreement of the said wardens and fower men." "Item...that no manne of their Crafte journeyman or other be attendant nor at the calling of anie gentleman, nor to noe other person otherwise than the lawe will but onlie to the wardens of their Crafte for the good rule of the same and assisting of the Bailiffs for keeping of the peace and for good rule of the Towne."

Mercers' Composition, 1480—81. The searcher is "to make serche and espye all suche p'sones as frawdelentlye abbrygg, w^{t}draw or cownceyle the payments of theyre dewties" (such as Toll, Murage, etc.).

No livery is to be worn except that of the Gild or Corporation. When the town bell rings the alarum members of the Gild are to go to the help of the Bailiffs only.

[1] Tailors' Composition, of 1478. Cf. *Eng. Gilds*, pp. 286, 385, 407, 420, etc.

[2] There are examples of the town drawing up trading ordinances to which the Gildsmen conformed. Cf. The Usages of Winchester and the Ordinances of Worcester in *Eng. Gilds*, pp. 349, 370. Cf. also pp. 334—337.

cognisance of trade affairs except indirectly through the Gilds; another was that the Gilds were supported by the town authorities. In order to carry out the rules of the Gilds it was imperative that all men of a trade should belong to the particular Gild of that craft. For there might come men carrying on trade in the town unwilling to submit to the rules framed for ensuring good work and protecting the interests of the craft. These it would be impossible to check until the Gild had been recognised and authorised by the crown or the corporation, and so had obtained power to enforce its ordinances in a legitimate way. It was in this manner that the necessity arose for obtaining a charter[1]. The Fraternities, which in their earlier stages had existed as voluntary associations, now received authoritative recognition, by virtue of charters obtained from the king by the aid of the corporation. The composition of the Tailors and Skinners (1478) shows the

shown by Charters, company and the corporation in the closest connection; that of the Mercers, granted by Edward Prince of Wales, Son of Edward IV., in 1480—81, is countersigned by the bailiffs.

The necessity for this authoritative recognition is clearly seen in the continually recurring ordinance calling upon all men of the craft to join the Gild. If the Gild had not been supported by royal and municipal authority it would have been impossible for it to have carried out its aims; as it was the task was sufficiently difficult.

---

[1] Also before they could hold land in mortmain it would be necessary to obtain a charter.

The unity of interests of the Gilds and the corporation is further shown by the words of the oaths. The wardens' oath of the company of *and Oaths.* Glovers ran as follows.

" You shalbe true to our Sov'aigne lord King
" ... his heirs and successors and obedient to
" the Bailiffs of this town for the time being
" and their successors. And you shall well and
" truly execute and p'forme your office of Wardens
" of Glovers, Poynt-makers, pursers, ffelmongers,
" Lethersellers and pa'hment-makers for this
" yeare according to the true extent and meaning
" of your composition and of all and singular
" articles and agreements therein expressed and
" declared to the uttermost of your power. So
" helpe you God."

The oaths of the other officers, and of the Freemen, contained like promises[1].

In the composition of the Trade Gilds there was *Composi-* no attempt to erect a monopoly. All workers of the *tion of Gilds.* Craft except such as could make separate terms with *Masters.* the corporation[2] were not only permitted to join the Gild, but were compelled to do so. The members *Appren-* included Apprentices and Journeymen as well as *tices. Journey-* Masters[3]. Women too were not debarred from *men.*

---

[1] The Oath of the Freemen of the Mercers' Company is given as a note to this Chapter.

[2] Cf. Appendix.

[3] " The position of master and journeyman was not that of capitalist and labourer, so much as that of two fellow-workers, one of whom, from his superior status, was responsible to the town for the conduct of both." Cunningham, 211. As showing

Women. joining[1], though they, like the Apprentices and Journeymen[2], took no part in the business of administration[3]. The charter of the Drapers[4] speaks of both brethren and sistren, and the list of members as given on the occasions of "cessments" shows women-members, both wives of combrethren, independent tradeswomen, and widows of deceased brothers.

Officers. In the election of their officers the English Gilds differed materially from similar associations on the continent. In England the choice appears to have been always unrestricted[5]. Refusal to accept office when elected exposed the reluctant brother to a money fine. The oaths of the officers, as we have seen, contained declarations of loyalty to the crown and municipal authority, and in this way we may account for the absence of *Masters* among the officials of the Shrewsbury Gilds. The place of the Master seems to have been filled, in some sort at least, by the bailiffs of the town. At any rate none

the position of an apprentice in the 15th century a Shrewsbury Indenture is given as a note to this Chapter.

[1] Cunningham, 211, n. 1. Brentano, 40, 68.

[2] "The Stock in Trade required to set up in business was not great and an apprentice when his term of service was over, became a master almost as a matter of course. Journeymen were scarce, or at any rate not plentiful enough to have much influence on Trade....Thus Capital and Labour were united." *Quarterly Review*, Vol. 159, p. 53.

[3] Brentano, 40.

[4] Merewether and Stephens.

[5] For interference with Free Election on the Continent cf. Brentano.

of the many Gilds of Shrewsbury ever had a Master at the head of their officers.

The *Wardens* were uniformly two in number, freely elected by all the brethren from such as were "the most worthiest and discreetest and which will and best can[1]." That it was not altogether a needless precaution to order that the elected wardens should be members of the Gild appears from the later abuses which arose, wardens being sometimes chosen from without the number of the combrethren[2]. The functions of these, the principal officers, were generally to carry into effect the objects of the Gild. To do this they possessed the right of search for inadequate materials or unsuitable tools, and a general supervision over workmen to secure competency. The composing of quarrels among combrethren was a prominent part of their duties.

The Board of Assistants which exercised so *Assistants.* harmful an influence over the companies in later days is found at Shrewsbury at an early date[3]. The composition of the Tailors and Skinners, 1478 A.D., speaks of the "Fower men ordeigned to the said Wardens to be assistant in counsel in

---

[1] Tailors' Composition, 1563.

[2] Cf. infra, Chap. VI.

[3] Cf. the four Auditors to superintend the accounts of the London Grocers (1348) and the six members who were chosen "to aid the Wardens in the discharge of their duties" (1397), of whom Mr George Howell says: "*Other than these, no notice of the existence of a committee or of assistants, in England, appears earlier than the sixteenth Century.*" *Conflicts of Capital and Labour*, p. 40. Brentano, p. 62. Cf. the four Assistants in the Merchant Gild of Ipswich, Gross, I. 24.

good counsel giving." They reappear in 1563 as the Four Assistants "for advising them [the Wardens] in the Government of the Gild[1]." In this particular as in so many others the Gilds of Shrewsbury seem to have been distinguished by a greater desire to widen the area of the governing body than was the case with the great companies of London and elsewhere. For the language of some bye-laws of the corporation passed in 18 Edward IV., seems to imply that the "Four Men" were common to all the companies. In the Gilds of most provincial towns such Assistants no doubt shared in the government from early years.

The *Stewards* were two in number. At a later date they were nominated by the Wardens[2], though in earlier times probably elective. Their particular duties nowhere very clearly appear. They seem to have assisted the Wardens and Four Men in hearing and examining of "all manner of matters, causes and controv'sies which shall happen amongst the brethren[3]."

The *Beadle* summoned members to meetings and officiated in whatever of formality was observed in them. He would keep the door of the Hall, and see that none but brethren were admitted within the privileged chamber. His was the duty of providing that due order and regularity was observed

[1] The "Four Men of Counsel" of the Mercers were, by the Composition of 1480—81, chosen by the Wardens.
[2] Mercers' Composition, 1480—81. Tailors' and Skinners', 1563.
[3] Tailors' Composition, 1563.

in the proceedings, and, if necessary, of carrying into effect the decisions of the assembly against refractory members. In the annual Procession we can well imagine that the Beadles of the respective companies would bear themselves with no common pride. Their duties also included the summoning of members to weddings and funerals of brethren.

The Mercers' composition of 1424 carefully details the duties of the *Searcher*. He, as also the Beadle, was usually nominated by the Wardens, Four Men and Stewards jointly, and, as his name implied, was charged with bringing to the notice of the Gild anything contrary to its rules or prejudicial to its interests.

A *Clerk* is also mentioned, who drew up indentures of apprenticeship and kept the Gild registers. At a later period the office of *Treasurer* was introduced and became of considerable importance.

The election of officers was the principal item of *Meetings.* business at the great annual meeting of the Gild. This was held on the festival of the Saint in whose name the Gild was dedicated. It was preceded by Mass in the Parish Church whither the brethren and sistren went in procession wearing their distinctive hoods and liveries, and bearing lights in their hands. To add to the dignity of the occasion a play or mystery was sometimes performed, but more usually such representations were reserved for the great common feast of Corpus Christi.

At the meeting, which from its most general name of "mornspeche" appears to have followed soon after Mass, great solemnity was observed. The

double-locked box[1] was opened by the two Wardens[2] amidst a reverential silence, and the composition or charter preserved in it rehearsed to the assembled *Business at* brethren. Business was then proceeded with :—elec-
meetings. tion of officers, admittance of new brethren, authorisation of indentures. Then if necessary regulations were passed for the government of the Gild and ordinances made for the due protection of trade, such as summonses to Intruders to enter the union.
Penalties. The ordinary penalties which the companies might inflict were fines of money or of wax, (in which king and corporation shared and which they were consequently willing to enforce,) and, in extreme cases total expulsion from the Gild, which of course meant exclusion from trade within the town.

After the " mornspeche " came the mutual feast. The brethren had begun the day by union for worship, they ended it with union for social and convivial festivity. In later times the business portion of the meeting was transacted in the Hall
Halls. of the Gild and the brethren afterwards adjourned to some convenient tavern. Several of the Halls were standing until quite recent times. Such were those of the Mercers, Tailors, and Weavers[3]. That of the Shearmen is now used as an Auction Mart, but the Drapers' Hall still retains its former dignity.

It will be necessary to attempt some estimation

[1] Several of these are in the Town Museum at Shrewsbury.

[2] A " Key-keeper " appears later in the lists of officers.

[3] Their situation is given in *Some account of the Ancient and Present state of Shrewsbury*, published in 1808.

of the extent and value of the influence which the *Necessity*
Gilds exercised on contemporary life and thought. *of his-*
torical
In doing this, and indeed in dealing with the whole *attitude*
subject of trade regulation in the Middle Ages, it is
necessary to bear continually in mind that not only
were the conditions of trade then very materially
different from those under which we now live, but
that Economic Theory was still more at variance with
modern views. It is necessary therefore to take a
historical attitude, and to try to appreciate both the
difference of social conditions, and the difference
of objects in view. These objects may be considered
firstly as individual and perhaps selfish; and, secondly,
as general and for the common good.

1. If we consider the charters from the first *in esti-*
point of view we see that the trade regulations *mating*
import-
were dictated by the desire to secure to all the *ance of*
brethren their means of livelihood: "no broder" *Gilds;*
Com-
was to "induce or tyce any other Mastres Ac- *mercial,*
costom," or to employ the servants of another combrother, or otherwise to act in a spirit of unbrotherly
and dishonourable competition. The charters are
full of such regulations. No member might obtrude
wares before passers in the open street, or erect
booths "for to have better sale than eny of the
combrethren[1]."

2. Similarly also if we view the compositions
in light of what we have described as the second
of their objects. The excellent motive of mediæval regulation of industry was to secure the prosperity of trade by ensuring skilled workmanship

[1] Barbers' Composition (1483 A.D.).

and proper materials. In consequence it was for-
bidden for workmen whose capacity was unknown to
work in the town until their efficiency had been
proved. The Barbers' composition of 1432 ordered
that "no man' p'sone sette up nother holde no shoppe
in Privite ny apperte ny shave as a Maistre withinne
the saide Tow' ny Franchise in to the Tyme that
ev'y such p'sone have the Wille and Assent of the
Stywardes and Maistres of the saide Crafte." It was
the desire to ensure the public being well served that
prompted the articles in the composition of the
Mercers (1480—1) which ordered the Searcher " to
make serche uppon all the occupyers of the saide
Craftes...that non of theym occupie eny false
Balaunce Weight or Mesures belongeing to the sayde
Craftes or eny of theym, wherebie the Kyngs People
in eny wyse myght be hurt or dysseyved." It was
also part of the same officer's duties to " oversee that
any thyng app'tenyng to the saide Craftes or eny of
theym to be boght and solde in the saide Towne and
Fraunceses be able suffyceant and lawfull and that
noe dyssayte nor gyle to the Kyngs liege people
therbye be had." No indentures were to be drawn
for less than "seven years at the least," so that
adequate training should be secured.

We thus perceive how the Craft Gilds differed,
on the one hand from the Frith Gilds of more ancient
times, and on the other from the Commercial Companies of later days. The former were associations
in which every member was responsible for the
actions of each of his fellows; in the Craft Gilds
each member bound himself to abide by the regula-

tions of the rest. The essence of the later Commercial Companies is union for mere pecuniary gain; the Gilds set in the forefront of the objects of their association the material benefit of the community and the religious and moral good of the individual. The resemblance between Trades Unions and the Mediæval Gilds is not entirely fanciful; but no two documents can be more widely different than the Prospectus of a Limited Liability Company and a Gild Charter of the Middle Ages.

The Gild system may be considered from various points of view. Regarded in its social aspect its *Social,* importance can hardly be exaggerated. It has been pointed out how the work of the Gilds prevented the difficulty of poor relief becoming acute, and also how valuable their influence was in the maintenance of order, through the respect they evinced for the established law. The immense weight they must have had on the side of morality, by the importance they attached to the moral character of their members must not be overlooked. "The rules of the Gilds which have come down to us, quaint and homely as they sound, breathe a spirit as elevated as it is simple, and although we must probably make the usual allowance for the difference between men's acts and their words, we cannot but believe that the generations which formed such grand conceptions and which so persistently strove to realise them, had a better side than posterity has discovered[1]."

The extent, too, to which they operated in linking

[1] *Quarterly Review*, Vol. 159, p. 44.

class to class was very great. There was no impassable barrier between commerce and birth. In the lists of apprentices which have been preserved to us the entries of names belonging to county families are frequent. It was the ordinary custom for the younger sons to be put to business in the town. The social value of such a habit must have been great. Within the craft, too, the distinctions were only caused by differences in the degrees of wealth. By industry and perseverance the meanest apprentice might look forward to the attainment of the highest honours his Gild could bestow, and even, by success in trade, to nobility. As in Athelstan's time the merchant who fared thrice beyond the sea at his own cost became of thegn-right worthy[1], so it was all through the Middle Ages: even in the 17th century Harrison says " our merchants do often change estate with gentlemen, as gentlemen do with them, by a mutual conversion of the one into the other[2]."

Constitutional. The education obtained by the framing of their own ordinances was also no slight gain to the townsmen. They provided for their peculiar needs in their own peculiar way, not always we may say in the best way, but in that which they, who knew the special requirements of the case, considered the best. Each who took part in drawing up those regulations would feel that a certain share of responsibility rested with him to see that they were kept. The constitutional importance also of this training, in imparting an appreciation of the responsibilities and

[1] *Select Charters*, p. 65. [2] *Elizabethan England*, p. 9.

duties which devolve on those who frame regulations was not unimportant.

The services which the Gilds rendered to the cause of liberty by the feeling of strong cohesion which they produced among the townsmen would be less difficult to estimate if the burgesses had played a more distinctive part in the work of Parliament[1]. It is easier to point out how, if they may have interfered to some extent with family life on the one hand, they on the other increased the tendency to narrowness and localism which was otherwise sufficiently strong throughout the Middle Ages, and indeed through considerably later times. Everything was antagonistic to the widening of the townsman's sympathies. He found his trade, his ambition, almost his whole life, satisfied within the walls of the borough in which he dwelt; and the Craft Gilds crystallised, as it were, this tendency towards insularity.

It may be noticed how a special interest attaches at the present time to the history of the Gilds and to the study of their influence and development. *Special interest of their history at present time.*

The condition of the working classes must always be a point of vital importance to the welfare of the state. It is peculiarly so to-day. Anything therefore which can assist us to understand how the present degradation of the craftsman has been brought about, and which may help towards his amelioration, will be valuable and of practical usefulness.

Five hundred years ago the working man differed

[1] Stubbs, *Constitutional History*, Vol. III., p. 607.

very widely from his modern representative; how widely may be gathered from a single illustration. The architects of the Churches and other buildings which the Middle Ages have bequeathed to us in such large numbers and of such exquisite beauty are, in the vast majority of cases, unknown to-day even by name. They were not less unknown to contemporaries. For they were men of like nature with their fellows: *ancestors of our modern artisans.* How great a change has grown up in the generations which have intervened.

Five centuries ago the workman was intelligent and skilled, he is now untrained and degraded: he was then able and accustomed to take a proper pride in his work, he is now careless and indifferent: he used to be provident and thrifty, now he is usually reckless and wasteful.

It is not too much to say that a great reason of this vast difference is to be found in the influence which the Gilds exercised. In their character as Benefit Clubs they taught their members to be thrifty: by insisting on a careful and systematic training during seven years of apprenticeship they made them skilled and capable workmen, and as such able to take an interest in, and to derive pleasure from their work. It has been pointed out that the Gilds prevented extreme poverty from ever becoming at all normal. Uncertainty of employment and de-moralising fluctuations of wages are among the most crying evils of our modern social *régime.* The Craft Gilds did much to secure regularity of work and to steady the price of labour.

Thus it is evident how great and peculiar an interest attaches to the whole subject of the Gilds at the present day. It is a subject which does not merely offer attractions to the antiquary or provide valuable materials for the student of constitutional and municipal development. It has a far wider and more human significance. A study of the extent and nature of the influence which the Gilds exercised on the condition and skill of the working man in the past will help to solve the problem of his improvement in the present and in the future.

NOTE I.

INDENTURE OF APPRENTICESHIP FROM THE MERCERS' COMPANY'S RECORDS. A.D. 1414.

Hæc Indentura testatur etc. inter Johannem Hyndlee de Northampton, Brasyer, et Gulielmum filium Thomæ Spragge de Salopia, quod predictus Gulielmus posuit semetipsum apprenticium dicto Johanni Hyndlee, usque ad finem octo annorum, ad artem vocatam *brasyer's craft*, quâ dictus Johannes utitur, medio tempore humiliter erudiendum. Infra quem quidem terminum præfatus Gulielmus concilia dicti Johannis Hyndlee magistri sui celanda celabit. Dampnum eidem Johanni nullo modo faciet nec fieri videbit, quin illud cito impediet aut dictum magistrum suum statim inde premuniet. A servicio suo seipsum illicite non absentabit. Bona et catalla dicti Johannis absque ejus licentiâ nulli accomodabit. Tabernam, scortum, talos, aleas, et joca similia non frequentabit, in dispendium magistri sui. Fornicationem nec adulterium cum aliqua muliere de domo et familia dicti Johannis nullo modo committet, neque uxorem ducet, absque licentia magistri sui. Præcepta et mandata licita et racionabilia magistri sui ubique pro fideli posse ipsius Gulielmi, diligenter adimplebit et eisdem mandatis libenter obediet. Et si prædictus Gulielmus de aliqua convencione sua vel articulo præscripto defecerit, tunc idem Gulielmus juxta modum et quantitatem delicti sui magistro suo satisfaciet emendam aut terminum apprenticiatus sui duplicabit.   Et præfatus Johannes et assignati sui apprenticium suum in arte prædicta meliori modo quo idem Johannes sciverit ac poterit tractabunt docebunt et informabunt, seu ipsum informari facient sufficienter, debito modo castigando, et non aliter.   Præterea dictus Johannes concedit ad docendum et informandum dictum Gulielmum in arte vocata *Peuterer's Craft* adeo bene sicut sciverit seu poterit ultra convencionem suam præmissam.   Et idem Johannes nullam partem artium prædictarum ab apprenticio suo concelabit.   Invenient insuper Johannes et assignati sui dicto Gulielmo omnia sibi necessaria, viz. victum suum et vestitum, lineum, laneum, lectum, hospicium, calceamenta et cætera sibi competencia annuatim sufficienter, prout ætas et status ipsius Gulielmi exigerint.   In cujus rei testimonium etc. 1414.

NOTE II.

OATH TO BE TAKEN BY THE FREEMEN OF THE MERCERS' COMPANY.

In the Company's records this oath occurs immediately after a curious calendar, written in 15th century hand, and before a list of "Brethren received and incorporated in the time of Rici Attynchin and John Cutlere wardens" in 3 Henry VI., (1424–5).

FIDELITAS.

I shall trewe man be to God o'r Lady Seynt Marie Seynt Mychell th'archangell patrone of the Gylde and to the Fraternite of the Mercers Yremongers and Goldsmythes & Cappers w'in the Towne and Fraunches of Shrowesbury I shall also Trewe man be to the king our liege lorde and to his heyres kyngys and his lawes and mynystars of the same Truly obs've and obey And ov' this I shall be obedyent to my wardens and their sumpneys obey and kepe I shall be trewe and ffeythfull to the Combrethern of the Gylde aforeseyd and ther co'ncell kepe All lawdable and lefull actes and composic'ons made or to be made w^tin the Seide Gylde truly obeye p'forme and kepe aft' my reason and power I shall be contributare bere yelde and paye all man' ordynare charges cestes and contribucons aftur my power as any other master occupyer or combrother of the seid Gylde shall happen to doe and bere: Soe helpe me God and halidame and by the Boke.

CHAPTER IV.

THE EARLY HISTORY OF THE GILDS OF SHREWSBURY.

IN the foregoing chapter it has been shown how the Craft Gilds were called into being. They possessed at first no charters[1] because none were needed. It was only when friction arose that there came any necessity for royal authority to step forward with its support and sanction[2]. *Existed before they held charters.*

And as they at first possessed no charters, so they have left few or no records of their earliest life. So long as they worked in thorough accord with the spirit of the age and completely fulfilled its requirements they left scanty traces. It is only when the period of degeneracy commences that we begin to have anything like adequate materials for their detailed history. *Scanty notice at first.*

[1] The writs issued in 1388 order returns of the "Charters and Letters Patent *si quas habent*": cf. Toulmin Smith, pp. 128, 130. The "Compositions" spoken of below were renewals and confirmations of previously enjoyed privileges. They usually assert that the Gild has been in existence "a tempore quo non extat memoria."

[2] Charters were also necessary before lands could be acquired in mortmain.

*Four-
teenth
century;
difficulties
for Gilds
to face.*

The 14th century was fruitful in illustrations of the difficulties which beset the work of the Gilds.

The development of trade alone had proceeded far enough to render their task already complicated : their difficulties were increased abnormally by the exceptional conditions of labour brought about by the Black Death. The Peasant Revolt compelled Parliament to take cognisance of industrial difficulties. In 1388, at its meeting at Cambridge, it was largely occupied with trade questions[1], and ordered the issue of writs to the sheriff of each county in England, commanding returns of all details as to the foundation, objects, and condition of both religious fraternities and Craft Gilds. These returns show that most of the Gilds obtained their charters during the 13th and the early years of the 14th centuries[2].

It does not appear that any legislation followed upon this parliamentary action, but provisions now begin to appear for the settlement of disputes between masters and workmen, and also between brethren of the Gild. So far the different classes of workmen had worked together in harmony upon the whole, but it could not fail that a severance or at least a marked diversity of interests should arise.

[1] Stubbs, ii. p. 504 and note 1.

[2] Toulmin Smith. Introduction, p. xxiv. It is from these returns that Mr Toulmin Smith has compiled his collection of ordinances of "English Gilds," which however comprise but a small portion of the whole, and throw little or no light on the working of the Craft Gilds. The documents have not yet been calendared, but they do not appear to contain anything relating to Shrewsbury.

Most important, as demonstrating that it was the *Develop-*
change in external circumstances, and not so much *ment of*
industry.
the internal degeneracy of the Gilds themselves,
which was causing the friction, are the evidences
which show that a great division of labour was in
progress[1]. In the 13th century the tailor and the
cloth-merchant sever their former connection : the
businesses of the tanner and of the butcher become
distinct branches of trade[2]. Similarly the tanner
and the shoemaker were made separate callings[3].
The same movement is still more clearly seen in the
disputes which arose between allied Gilds as to the
particular work which each was charged with supervising[4]. It was the creation of opposing interests, of
which such were the outward signs, that introduced
the seed of decay into the Gild system.

How rapidly the degeneracy proceeded may be *Fifteenth*
gathered from a petition of the Commons early in *century :*
the 15th century (1437), which evoked an Act (15
Hen. VI., cap. 6) definitely recognising the existence *avowal of*
of abuses. After reciting how the *abuses,*

> " masters, wardens, and people of Gilds, frater-
> " nities, and other companies corporate, dwelling
> " in divers parts of the realm, oftentimes by
> " colour of rule and governance to them granted
> " and confirmed by charters and letters patent
> " ......made among themselves many unlawful
> " and little reasonable ordinances......for their

---

[1] Cunningham, p. 210, 211.
[2] Green, *Short History*, p. 192.
[3] Cunningham, p. 214.
[4] Brentano, 75 : Riley, *Memorials*, 539, 565, 568, 570, 571, &c.

"own singular profit and to the common hurt
"and damage of the people,"
the statute proceeded to order that the Gilds should
not in the future

"make or use any ordinance in disparity or
"diminution of the franchises of the king or
"others, or against the common profit of the
"people, nor allow any other ordinance if it is
"not first approved as good and reasonable by
"the Justices of the Peace or the chief Magis-
"trates aforesaid and before them enrolled and
"to be by them revoked and repealed afterwards
"if they shall be found and proved to be little
"loyal and unreasonable."

*but ap-
proval
of the
system.*

But it is abundantly clear that the complaints
are against the abuses of the system and not against
the system itself. Dissatisfaction is expressed at
the "little reasonable ordinances" of the Gilds but

*Policy of
Reform.*

not against the companies themselves. The policy
therefore of Henry VI. and Edward IV. was to reform
the Gilds by amending their ordinances, or, if necessary, giving them charters of incorporation which
should set forth definitely their objects, and state
both the extent and the limitation of their powers.
It is from this period that we date most of the
existing records of the Shrewsbury companies.
The barbers are said to have been chartered by
Edward I. in 1304[1]; their earliest extant composition[2] is dated 1432 (10 Hen. VI.). The Shoemakers' composition of 1387 recited a charter of

[1] Pidgeon's *Gilds of Shrewsbury*; *S. A. S.*, Vol. v. p. 265.
[2] *S. A. S.*, Vol. v. p. 266.

Edward III.[1] A Vintners' company is said to have
been erected in Shrewsbury by Henry IV. in 1412[1].

But it is with the accession of Henry VI. that the
great number of present charters and compositions
begins. The date of the Fishmongers' company is
1423[1], and the entries of the Mercers commence in
the next year[1]. The Barbers' composition of 1432
has been already mentioned. Then follow the
Weavers (1448–9), the Fletchers (1449), the Carpen-
ters (1449–50) in close proximity[1]. The Tailors and
Skinners (1461) were recognised in the last year of
Henry VI.[1], and eighteen years subsequently received
a new composition from Edward IV. (1478), who
had in the first year of his reign united the Fraternity of the Blessed Trinity with the company of the
Drapers[2]. The companies of the Millers, Bakers,
Cooks, Butchers and Shearmen certainly existed
before 1478, as they are mentioned as taking part
in the Corpus Christi Procession at that date. In
that year the Tanners and Glovers were incorporated[3],
as also were the Saddlers[3]. The royal recognition of
the Mercers[1] in the next year completed the list of
Shrewsbury companies erected before the 16th century.

It will be convenient here to draw attention to a *Later*
different kind of Gild which was founded in Shrews- *Religious*
bury towards the close of this period: the religious *Gilds.*
Gild of S. Winifred.

The ancient Monks' Gilds which had spread so

1 Pidgeon's *Gilds.*
2 Merewether and Stephens. Pidgeon's *Gilds.*
3 Pidgeon's *Gilds*; *S. A. S.* Vol. x. p. 33.

early over England, found as was to be expected later imitators in large numbers. The oldest accounts of these Gilds also, like those of the Monks' Gilds, are found in England[1]. Religious or Social they are usually called. They all evinced a strong religious character, but in addition had a care for the old and needy. If a Gild-brother suffer loss through theft "let all the Gildship avenge their comrade," says the Cambridge statute. They also took cognisance of public welfare. If a Gild-brother do wrong "let all bear it: if one misdo, let all bear alike." If a man be slain in fair quarrel with a Gild-brother the *wite* is to be borne by all, but the wilful or treacherous murderer is "to bear his own deed."

These Gilds rapidly spread over all Europe, and existed probably in every town. They doubtless formed the model to which the later associations looked, and, except in details, differed little from the Craft Gilds. They were frequently connected with trade, even in some instances consisting entirely of followers of specific crafts[2], and loans were made out of the common chest to help members in misfortune[3]. We have scant information of early religious Gilds in Shrewsbury, though there can be but little doubt they flourished there as elsewhere. Later, in the 15th century, one was founded by the Abbot of the Holy Cross, which presents several unusual and interesting features.

---

[1] Those of Abbotsbury, Cambridge and Exeter. Cf. supra, p. 9.
[2] Toulmin Smith, pp. 29, 42, &c.
[3] *Ibid.*, 7, 8, 11, &c.

Thomas Mynde was elected Abbot on January 8th, 1460, but it was not till 1486 that he took measures to found the Fraternity of S. Winifred, though probably the scheme had been previously shaping itself through the long period of unsettlement which the Civil Wars had caused. The present Gild differed from the earlier foundations in being deliberately created by royal charter. The reason was that without such security it could not receive grants of land, and Abbot Mynde was desirous to bequeath to it his private possessions rather than to leave them to his Monastery,—a curious commentary perhaps on the low estimation into which the religious houses had fallen.

The royal charter was not obtained without some trouble. The License itself says it was granted "by [reason of] the sincere devotion which we have and bear towards S. Winefrida Virgin and Martyr;" but Abbot Mynde assures us that this laudable zeal required the practical stimulus of "a large sum of money" before it would take effect in action.

The terms of the charter allowed both brethren and sisters to join the fellowship, the number being unregulated. The oath to support the Gild was taken by each member on admittance, kneeling before the altar in the Abbey of the Holy Cross. Power was given for the election of a Master, whose duties were the regulation of the Gild and the supervision of its property. The fraternity had its common seal, and the ordinary powers and privileges of corporations. It was especially exempted from the Mortmain Acts, and was allowed to acquire property to the yearly value of £10. The objects to which this was to be devoted were the finding of two Chaplains, or at least one, whose duties were the saying of a daily Mass at the Altar of S. Winifred in the Abbey, and the celebration of a Requiem Mass on the decease of a brother or sister of the Fraternity. At such Masses it was especially provided that the prayers for the departed soul should be *in English*.

The Gild was joined in considerable numbers by the principal folk of the town, but there is little information[1] respecting its history, which may be at once anticipated here. At the confiscation of the Chantry and Gild property the fraternity of S. Winifred was not able to plead the excuse of usefulness for trade purposes, and it fell unnoticed in the ruin of the great Abbey with which it was connected. Its life had been a short one, but coming as it did at a time when religious fervour was weak and morality lax, it no doubt served a useful purpose and deserved a better fate than almost total oblivion.

Charters granted to Craft Gilds. Returning after this digression to the Craft Gilds it will be interesting and profitable to make an examination and comparison of two of their charters, one selected from the earlier and one from the later portion of the period. The charter[2] of the Barbers' Gild, granted by Henry VI. in 1432, may be placed beside the composition[3] which Edward IV. gave to the Mercers in 1480.

[1] The little that is known about it is given in Owen and Blakeway's *History of Shrewsbury*, II. 122.

[2] It is printed in *S. A. S.*, Vol. v.

[3] *S. A. S.*, Vol. VIII.

A point which strikes us forcibly on the most *Religious* superficial examination of the charters, is the *articles.* prominence given, in one as in the other, to the Corpus Christi procession. It is a striking illustration of the extent to which mediæval materialism had permeated society, and how deeply rooted was that "tendency to see everything in the concrete, to turn the parable into a fact, the doctrine into its most literal application[1]," which scholastic philosophy had nurtured. The procession indeed would almost appear, from the charters, to be the principal object for which the Gilds exist. A considerable share of the fines is expressly devoted to the "Increce of the Lyght that is boren yerely in the heye and worthie ffest of Corpus Xti Day." The Mercers' composition regulates the order of the procession and the weight of the candle which the company provides in it. No member is to be out of his place on the festival without permission, and the combrethren are especially prohibited from going to "the Coventrie Fayre" at this season under penalty of a fine of twelve pence. The fact of being enabled to take part in the procession is manifestly looked upon as one of the great privileges and duties of the companies.

The Mercers' Gild also provided for a priest to say a daily Mass at the altar of S. Michael in the Church of S. Chad; and thirteen poor Bedesmen were retained at a penny per week to pray for the King and Queen and Councillors, and for the brethren of the Gild "both quyke and dedd."

The trade regulations of the two compositions

[1] Bryce, *Holy Roman Empire*, p. 95.

are naturally cast in the same mould. In both appears the prohibition of foreign labour (the Mercers say "except in fayre tyme"), and of under-selling by combrethren as well as unfair competition generally. The later regulations go further and provide for the carrying out of the ordinances of the composition by the appointment of a searcher to secure the use of good materials and to prevent "dissayte and gyle," the use of false weights, &c. They also forbid the taking of aliens as apprentices[1].

All indentures are to be for seven years at the least, and none are to be taken as apprentices with-out being properly bound by indentures approved by the wardens and recorded by the clerk. There is also the article which now becomes common, against divulging the secrets of the craft, and an interesting one against "eny confederacye or em-bracerye wherebie any p'judices hurt or hynd'ance myght growe."

Articles of reform. In the later charter, too, it is evident that there had arisen no small need for reform. In the fore-front it is stated that the previous "Fines assessyd uppon ev'y App'ntice at their entries to be maysters Combrethyrn and Settursuppe of the said Craftes or any of them," "and in like wyse gret Fynes uppon eny Forreyn that shoulde entre into the same" are "thought overchargeable" and so are to be "dymy-nished and refowrmed." If members refuse to pay them, as thus amended, they may be levied by

[1] "None that is of Frenshe, Flemmyshe, Irysh, Dowche, Walshe, or any other Nacyones borne not beyng at Truse w^t our Sov'ayne Lorde the kynge, but onlye mere Englysshe borne."

distress. Of how great a falling-off from the original spirit of brotherhood do these two short articles speak.

Both the documents provide for the trial of *Police.* dissensions among brethren, in preference to going before the ordinary tribunals, though by permission cases might be taken before the bailiffs of the town.

In a similar spirit of pacification the Mercers' *Liveries.* composition forbids the wearing of liveries "saving the lyverray of gownes or hodes of the said Gylde to be ordeyned and worne," and that of the municipal corporation[1]. This was in accordance with the Act 13 Henry IV. cap. 3. The abuse of liveries had evoked from Parliament an attempt to put a total stop to the custom[2] (13 Rich. II.). Such endeavours were futile. This was at last recognised, and in 13 Henry IV. the use of liveries of cloth was prohibited, but with the important proviso, "Gilds and fraternities and crafts in the cities and boroughs within the kingdom which are founded and ordained to good intent and purpose alone being excepted." In 1468 Edward IV. confirmed previous legislation on the subject[3].

In spite of reforms by improved compositions and *Sixteenth* legislative measures the degeneracy of the Gilds *century.* proceeded apace. The statute 19 Hen. VII. cap. 7

---

[1] Such Articles against the wearing of Liveries were common in the Gild Statutes. Cf. Toulmin Smith, *passim.*

[2] Except by the Nobility to their personal dependents. Cf. Stubbs, iii. 552.

[3] 8 Edw. IV. c. 2.

repeats the complaint of 15 Hen. VI. cap. 6, and re-enacts the same restrictions. "Divers and many ordinances have been made by many and divers private bodies corporate within cities, towns, and boroughs contrary to the King's prerogative, his laws, and the common weal of his subjects:" in future therefore the Gilds are prohibited from making any new by-laws or ordinances concerning the prices of wares and other things "in disheritance or diminution of the prerogative of the King, nor of other, nor against the common profit of the people, but that the same Acts or Ordinances be examined and approved by the Chancellor, Treasurer of England, or Chief Justices." The repetition of the same articles shows how little effective they had been in checking the abuses against which they were directed.

Policy of reform pursued. Nevertheless Henry VII. and Henry VIII. persevered in the work of regulating, reforming and strengthening the Gilds. The statute of 1530[1] once more diminished entrance fees, which had been inordinately and illegally raised; but another of 1536[2] repeating the same prohibition shows the utter futility of such measures in the condition of trade which had been brought about.

A more serious abuse appears in the latter statute, namely the attempt of the masters to exact from their apprentices an oath promising to refrain from prosecuting trade on their own account with-

[1] 22 Hen. VIII. c. 4. The Entrance Fees for Apprentices had been raised in some cases to 30/- and 40/-. They are now reduced to 2/6 Entrance Fee, and 3/4 Fee on taking up freedom.

[2] 28 Hen. VIII. c. 5.

out consent of their late master. Such abuses exhibit the Gilds in a state of wholesale demoralisation.

This was not unnatural under the circumstances, *Reformation.* for the course of the Reformation had tended to turn public opinion against the Gilds. Moreover it now gave them a severe shock on one side, at any rate, of their functions.

The confiscation of monastic lands had shown *Confiscation of Chantries and robbery of Gilds.* how easy it was for a needy government to seize upon corporate property to its own use, and the example was not long without being followed. The statute 37 Hen. VIII. cap. 4 gave the whole property of all Colleges, Hospitals, Fraternities and Gilds to the king. Before this wholesale desolation could be effected Henry died, but Somerset obtained a renewal[1] of the grant to Edward VI.

The words of the Act are absolute in making over to the king all the lands and other possessions of Chantries, Colleges, Hospitals, Gilds and bodies of a similar nature, both religious and secular. No distinction is made as to aim or object, utility or abuse. According to the terms of the statute, we should expect every Gild and corporate body in the country to come to an end with the years 1547—8. Nevertheless though the Chantries were seized the Craft Gilds in general remained. The reason for this apparent divergence between the provisions of the statute and the facts of the case is given by Burnet .

---

[1] 1 Edw. VI. cap. 14.

[2] *Hist. of Reformation*, II. 72.

Two parties opposed the passing of the Act.
Cranmer and the best of the Reformers were grieved
to see the material supports of the Church one after
another torn away to prop up the failing fortunes of
needy and rapacious courtiers. They desired to preserve the lands of the Chantries till the king came
of age, when they hoped they might be devoted to the
suitable object of augmenting the livings which had
been in such numbers impoverished by the Reformation changes. On the other hand were the burgesses.
These had no mind to see their own property confiscated, and their benefit societies and clubs sud-
denly broken up. We may appreciate the feelings
of the nation respecting the proposed measure by
considering what would be the effect of a statute
taking over the properties of all benefit clubs,
Trades Unions, Lodges of Oddfellows and Foresters,
and similar associations, to day.

Cranmer and his supporters failed to overthrow
the measure in the Lords, but when it came to the
lower house it was at once evident that a considerable amount of careful statesmanship and astute
policy would be requisite if the statute was to pass.
Apparently no opposition was expected, as the bill
was already engrossed, or perhaps it was hoped that
it might be smuggled through amidst the hurry of
the closing session. But the government discovered
that they had gone to the length of the nation's
patience. The Commons saw in its true enormity
the conspiracy of the rich and powerful against the
weak and poor, and this once perceived a check
was given, tardy but not quite too late, to the

long and disastrous course of spoliation and confiscation.

The opposition to the bill was obstinate, especially
as regarded that portion which dealt with the Gilds.
Led by the members for Lynn and Coventry the
house showed unmistakeably that it was at length
determined to submit no longer.   In fact the feeling
was evidently so strong that the government perceived the absolute necessity of drawing back.   The
mode in which this was done is explained in the
following extract, which, though written from the
court point of view, shows up the whole incident as
a choice specimen of the statesmanship of the period.

" Whereas in the last Parliament holden at West-
minster in November the first year of the King's
Majesty's reign, among other articles contained in
the Act for colleges and chantry lands, etc., to be
given unto his Highness, it was also insisted that
the lands pertaining to all guilds and brotherhoods
within this realm should pass unto his Majesty by
way of like gift: At which time divers there being
of the Lower House did not only reason and arraign
against that article made for the guildable lands, but
also incensed many others to hold with them, amongst
the which none were stiffer, nor more busily went
about to impugn the said Article than the burgesses
for the town of Lynn in the county of Norfolk and
the burgesses of the city of Coventry in the county
of Warwick.......In respect of which their allegations
and great labours made herein unto the House such
of his Highness's Council as were of the same House
there present, thought it very likely that not only

that Article for the guildable lands should be clashed, but also that the whole body of the Act might either sustain peril or hindrance, being already engrossed, and the time of the Parliament's prolongation hard at hand, unless by some good policy the principal speakers against the passing of that article might be stayed. Whereupon they did participate the matter with the Lord Protector's grace and other of the Lords of his Highness's Council: who pondering on the one part how the guildable lands throughout this realm amounted to no small yearly value, which by the article aforesaid were to be accrued to his Majesty's possessions of the Crown; and on the other part weighing in a multitude of free voices what moment the labours of a few settlers had been of heretofore in like cases, thought it better to stay and content them of Lynn and Coventry by granting to them to have and enjoy their guild lands etc. as they did before, than through their means, on whose importance, labour, and suggestions the great part of the Lower House rested, to have the article defaced, and so his Majesty to forego the whole lands throughout the realm. And for these respects, and also for avoiding of the promise which the said burgesses would have added for the guilds to that article, which might have ministered occasion to others to have laboured for the like, they resolved that certain of his Highness's Councillors, being of the Lower House, should persuade with the said burgesses of Lynn and Coventry to desist from further speaking or labouring against the said article, upon promise to them that if they meddled no further against it, his Majesty once having the guildable lands granted unto him by the Act...should make them over a new grant of the lands pertaining then unto their guilds etc. to be had and used to them as before: which thing the Councillors did execute, as was desired, and thereby stayed the speakers against it, so as the Act passed with the clause for the guildable lands accordingly[1]."

This remarkable document, which Canon Dixon *Import-* printed for the first time, is of surpassing interest, *ance of* not only to the historian of the Craft Gilds but also *the Oppo-* to the student of constitutional history. The un-*sition.* scrupulous recourse of the government to jobbery and corruption is not more revolting than the evidence of the increasing constitutional power of the Commons is interesting. It is evident from the account that when the country was with the house of Commons the voice of the latter could not be disregarded.

The upshot was that an understanding was entered into, to the effect that the Gild lands were to be only surrendered *pro formâ*, and that they should not in fact be confiscated. In most cases this arrangement was adhered to, and when the great crisis was past it was seen that the Gilds had lost their Chapels and Chantries with the fittings of these, but that their other possessions remained to them.

It has been pointed out how the increasing con- *Need of* stitutional power of the Commons could make itself *caution.* felt when the opinion of the nation was at its back.

[1] May, 1548 ; Council Book MS. in the Privy Council Office. Cf. Dixon, *Hist. of Church of Eng.* Vol. II. page 462, note.

That it undoubtedly was so at the present juncture
cannot be doubted.   The method which was adopted
for carrying out the provisions of the Act demon-
strates fully how violently the country had been
excited by the measure and by the danger to which
the Gild lands had been exposed.   The usual way of
putting such an Act into execution would have been
to send down commissioners to take particulars of
the Gilds and Chantries and of their possessions.
But royal commissioners had come to be looked
upon, not without ample reason, as merely the
formal heralds of state robbery.   If therefore such
commissioners were now sent out to manage the
dissolution of the Chantries and Hospitals it was
feared that disturbance would arise beyond the
power of the government to manage.   The more
politic plan was therefore adopted of enlisting the
people themselves in the cause as much as might be.

Injunc-
tions.
Injunctions[1] were issued "to the Parson, Vicar,
Curat, Chaunter, Priests, Churchwardens, and two
of the most honest Persons of the Parish of
being no Founders, Patrons, Donors, Lessees, nor
Farmers of the Promotions of Corporations hereafter
recited."

These, or four of them, were to make a return as
to the number of "Chantries, Hospitals, Colleges,
Free Chapels, Fraternities, Brotherhoods, Guilds and
Salaries, or Wages of Stipendiary Priests" in their
parish, together with all particulars as to the revenues, ordinances, objects, abuses, names and titles
of the same.   Full lists were to be drawn up of the

[1] Burnet, *Hist. of Reformation*, IV. 281.

lands and possessions of the Chantries, Colleges, and Gilds, and enquiry was instituted respecting any recent dissolutions or alienations which might have been made in prospect of the recent Act.

The contingency alluded to in the last article has sufficed to provide some writers with an excuse for the measure destroying the Chantries. No doubt the shock which the action of Henry VIII. in reference to the monasteries had given to all forms of corporate property had led many of the Gilds to attempt the realization of their property. All such transactions were to be null and void.

Accordingly the commissioners went down to each town and hamlet and took full particulars of all matters concerning the Gilds and Chantries. "All such as have enye vestments or other goods of the Coᵧ [of Mercers are ordered] to bring them in," in order to be sold, with the rest of the Chantry fittings, "to the most p' fitt." The fate of the other kinds of property held by the Gilds, such that is as could not be definitely made out to have been intended for the support of obits and the maintenance of lights, *Gilds too* seems to have depended considerably on fortuitous *powerful and* circumstances. In each individual case the Gild *popular* had to secure for itself the best terms it could. *to be wholly* Sometimes its property was obtained by the town, *destroyed.* either by grant or by purchase[1]. At Shrewsbury the almshouses of the Drapers and Mercers survived[2],

----

[1] Cf. Gross, i. 162, ii. 14, 170, 279.

[2] The Statute 14 Eliz. c. 14 was enacted "For the assurance of gifts, grants etc. made and to be made to and for the relief of the poor in the Hospitals etc."

and the vicar of S. Almond's Church in the
same town still receives the yearly sum which the
Shearmen settled on the chaplain they maintained
in that church.

As for the object which the Act itself alleged to
have been the motive for the destruction of the
Chantries, namely the desire on the part of the
government to devote the revenues to the foundation and improvement of grammar schools, it was
forgotten as soon as parliament had separated.
Strype[1] is obliged to confess that the Act was
"grossly abused, as the Act in the former King's
reign for dissolving religious houses was. For
though the public good was pretended thereby
(and intended too, I hope), yet private men, in
truth, had most of the benefit, and the King and
Commonwealth, the state of learning, and the condition of the poor, left as they were before, or worse.
Of this, great complaints were made by honest men :
and some of the best and most conscientious preachers
reproved it in the greatest auditories, as at Paul's
Cross, and before the King himself. Thomas Lever,
a Fellow, and afterwards Master of St John's College
in Cambridge, in a sermon before the King, in the
year 1550 showed 'how those that pretended, that
(beside the abolishing of superstition) with the lands
Perversion of abbeys, colleges, and chantries, the King should be
of the con-
fiscated enriched, learning maintained, poverty relieved, and
revenues. the Commonwealth eased, purposely had enriched
themselves....And bringing in grammar schools,
which these dissolved chantries were to serve for

1 *Memorials*, Vol. II. Part I. page 100.

the founding of, he told the King plainly...many grammar schools, and much charitable provision for the poor, be taken, sold and made away; to the great slander of you and your laws, to the utter discomfort of the poor, to the grievous offence of the people, to the most miserable drowning of youth in ignorance....The King bore the slander, the poor felt the lack. But who had the profit of such things, he could not tell. But he knew well, and all the world saw, that the Act made by the King's Majesty and his Lords and Commons of his Parliament, for maintenance of learning and relief of the poor, had served some as a fit instrument to rob learning, and to spoil the poor.'" The measure was indeed an act of spoliation devoid either of excuse in its cause or benefit in its results. The suppression of the Monasteries could doubtless be amply excused, but no real justification is possible for this attempted wholesale seizure of institutions founded and maintained for the benefit of the poor, for the relief of suffering, and for the regulation of industry and police. As regards the last—the regulation of industry and police—the attempt was to a certain extent foiled, but in other respects it succeeded only too well. Even on the Gilds which escaped its effects were disastrous. Their spiritual aspect was taken away; *Disastrous* their prestige and authority very materially lessened. *effects on* *Gilds,* For they completely changed their nature. Instead of being brotherhoods of workmen,—masters, journeymen, and apprentices,—striving together for the common good, they now became simply leagues of employers, companies of capitalists. The new powers which the masters obtained were used to still further oppress the craftsman, who was sufficiently degraded *and on* already through a variety of causes. He was too poor *Craftsmen.* and powerless to be able to take any part in the new companies, and continued to sink deeper and deeper into degradation and misery. And this, too, in spite of the great and rapid development of trade which came simultaneously with this weakening blow at the authority and stability of the Gilds. Shrewsbury participated in this expansion of industry, and in the latter portion of the sixteenth century was peculiarly prosperous. There was no migration of its trade to the freer air of the neighbouring villages. The town was successful in retaining its monopoly.

But these two causes, (i) the weakening of the Gilds and their change of character, and (ii) the vast development of trade which the age was witnessing, combined to render the companies which survived the Reformation quite unable to perform the work which the mediæval Gilds had done. Yet then above all was a controlling and a guiding power essential. Elizabeth in consequence found that one of her first measures must be in remedy of this condition of affairs.

CHAPTER V.

REORGANISATION OF THE GILD-SYSTEM.

ELIZABETH, on her accession, found that imme- *Reign of* diate reform was imperative in almost every depart- *Elizabeth.* ment of state. The whole trade of the country was in a condition of agitation. Everything seemed unsettled and insecure.

For the social upheaval which the Reformation had brought about came in the train of a long period of economic disorder. The changes in the mode of *Economic* cultivation had thrown the mass of the country *dis-* population out of work. These were driven in large *turbances* numbers by stress of circumstances into the towns, which were consequently overstocked with hands. At this juncture came the breaking down of the social police within the towns by the weakening of the Gilds, while in the rural districts the dissolution of the monasteries took away from the poor their main hope of sustenance. The evils which such a policy of mere destruction must inevitably have brought upon the nation were averted through the national growth of wealth which the same period had witnessed. In the country parts the ejection of the easy-going old abbots had at least favoured the adoption of newer and improved methods of cultivation, so that a greater number of labourers came in *and in-* time to be required on the estate[1]. But far more *dustrial* satisfactory for absorbing the surplusage of labour *activity.* was the development which the period witnessed in manufacture. The woollen trade in the west, the worsted trade in the east, the iron trade in the south, and unmistakeable signs of the cloth trade in the north already showed how the foundations of England's wealth were laid.

The writers of the period abound in notices of the unparalleled growth of trade and commerce. Harrison laments "that every function and several vocation striveth with other, which of them should have all the water of commodity ran into her own cistern[2]." Ample openings for capital broke through the old prejudices against the taking of interest. "Usury" as it was called—"a trade brought in by the Jews—is now perfectly practiced almost by every Christian, and so commonly that he is accompted but for a fool that doth lend his money for nothing[3]." The English workman too was growing rich and lazy in the sunlight of prosperous times, so that "strangers" were frequently preferred to native craftsmen as "more reasonable in their takings, and less wasters of time by a great deal than our own[4]."

---

[1] Against this were to be set the "enclosing" and "non-residence" grievances.

[2] *Elizabethan England*, p. 11.

[3] *Ibid.*, p. 121.   [4] *Ibid.*, p. 117.

This was the commencement of the period of Shrewsbury's greatest prosperity. Edward IV.'s erection of the Court of the President and Marches of Wales (1478) was a material cause of the advent of peace to the Borders. Henry VII. could gratify national sentiment by tracing his descent from Owen Tudor: he gave it a practical turn by placing his son Arthur at Ludlow as ruler of the principality. The Welshmen had thus begun to feel that their union with England was a real one before Henry VIII. finally incorporated the country with the English kingdom.

The cessation of Welsh distractions had greatly favoured the advancement of Shrewsbury. Its grammar school—founded by Edward VI.—as the entrance register of Thomas Ashton, its first Head-master, evidences, attracted scholars from a very wide area, and helped to bring renown and wealth to the town. Shrewsbury too was the market to which the Welsh cloth trade naturally gravitated, though the town had powerful rivals with which to contend. In the reign of Elizabeth it employed six hundred shearmen in the woollen industry. Camden, writing in 1586, describes it as "a fine city, well-inhabited and of good commerce, and by the industry of the Citizens is very rich." From *Increase* this period date the substantial homes of the trades- *of comfort.* men of Tudor times which still survive in not inconsiderable numbers to give so much picturesqueness to the streets of the town. This was the era of improvements in domestic architecture. "If ever curious building did flourish in England," says

Harrison[1], "it is in these our years." Ireland's mansion, which dates from 1570, and the house at the south-east corner of the Market Square, built by John Lloyd in 1579, are existing examples of this "curious building." Their elegance, no less than their stability, betokens the advancement of manners as well as of wealth. Though these houses are "yet for the most part of strong timber" "brick or hard stone[2]" were beginning to be largely used. Rowley's mansion (1618) is said to have been the first house in the town built wholly of these materials.

Everything combines to mark the reign of Elizabeth as an epoch in the history of England. The foundations of modern society were laid. We seem to come into the range of modern, as distinct from mediæval ideas and habits. The principal points in which modern society differs from mediæval are distinctly visible. The problem of poor relief in particular becomes acutely appreciated. The rise of capital is seen both in the modification of the Usury laws, spoken of above, and in the enhancing of rents: prices hitherto dependent on custom and regulation must now be decided by competition.

Economic policy.

Not less remarkable is the permanence which attended Elizabeth's legislation. Her economic settlement remained practically unchanged until the development of machinery altered those social conditions for which it had been adapted.

---

[1] *Elizabethan England*, p. 117.
[2] *Ibid.*

She made trade regulation national instead of *The Statute 5 Eliz. a turning-point in Gild history.* local. The Act of 5 Elizabeth, c. 14, is a turning-point in the history of the Gilds. By it the whole system of Gilds was re-modelled. Their experience was by no means thrown away[1]. The information they had been accumulating was now appropriated by the state, which took over many of the functions they had hitherto performed.

What had long been common law now became *Many of the functions of the Gilds taken over by the state.* statute law. The old minimum of seven years' apprenticeship was still enjoined as a necessary preliminary to the exercise of any craft. Such apprentices when bound must be of an age less than twenty-one years, and could only be bound to householders in corporate or market towns. The proportion of journeymen to apprentices was regulated: there were to be three apprentices to one journeyman. The workman was protected from wilful dismissal. The hours of labour were defined, and Justices of the Peace or the town magistrates were to assess wages yearly at the Easter Sessions. All disputes between masters and servants were to be settled by the same authorities. The statute in-

[1] The good work of the Gilds is expressly acknowledged in many charters of the time, e.g. the charter granted to Faversham (1616) recites that long experience had shown that the dividing of the government of towns into several companies had worked great good, and was the means of avoiding many inconveniences and preposterous disorders, in respect that the government of every artificer and tradesman being committed to men of gravity, best experienced in the same faculty and mystery, the particular grievances and deceits in every trade might be examined, reformed and ordered. Gross, II. 89.

corporated everything that was worth taking in the
ordinances of the Gilds and applied it nationally to
the regulation of the country's trade.

*Trade-
regulation
becomes
national
instead of
local.*

*This
allows de-
velopment
of new
centres*

The results of such a revolution in industrial
regulation were great both on trade in general and
on the Gilds.   There was no longer any excuse for
attempting to retard the development of the new
centres which were springing up.   The action of the
government in the matter of the Welsh woollen
trade to which reference will presently be made
shows how its policy was tending more and more
towards allowing industry to take its own course,
instead of attempting to restrict it to one market.

*and
encourages
native
workmen.*

Another important result of the Act was the
protection henceforth shown to the native in opposition to the alien workman.   The aim of the
government is now to regulate, protect, encourage,
native industry : the objects of its desire in the past
had been to provide plenty for the consumer and to
increase the strength of the country by extending
its capacity for production.   The royal support accorded in consequence to Flemish and German
traders had made them objects of bitter jealousy
to the struggling English merchants[1].   This feeling
of antipathy to alien workmen may be traced from
the reign of Richard II.   It becomes very marked
in that of Edward IV.[2]   The composition of the
Mercers of Shrewsbury, dated 1480–81, had for-
bidden the apprenticeship of anyone "that is of
Frenshe, Flemyshe, Irysh, Douche, Walshe or eny

[1] Cunningham, p. 181.
[2] Cf. especially, 3 Edw. IV. c. 4 ; 22 Edward IV. c.

other Nacyones not beyng at Truse w^t our Sov'ayne
Lorde the Kynge, but onlye mere Englysshe borne."

The new policy inaugurated by the statute of
Elizabeth is however not more national in its scope
than in the preference it gives to native over foreign
workmen.

The results on the Gilds were more diverse. *Results on Gilds.* Many came to an end. This was brought about *Many come to an end.* through two causes: firstly, the need for many Gilds ceased in consequence of the government *Many made more comprehensive.* now taking over their functions; secondly, in many places the numerous Gilds were organized and amalgamated into one or two larger and amended corporations[1]. On the other hand the encouragement now afforded to native workmen caused a great incorporation of new trades into many old Gilds, which became in consequence more comprehensive. In a large number of cases these performed their duties well for a long period. The new composition granted to the Barbers of Shrewsbury in 1662 places this fact upon record. Occasionally they came in *These sometimes come into conflict with royal officers.* conflict with the royal officers appointed to scrutinise the wares, as was the case with the Mercers and the Anager at one period of the company's existence.

Not a few became the authorised agents of *Many become state agents.* the state. Several of the Shrewsbury Gilds were strengthened and encouraged with this object in view. New compositions were granted by Elizabeth to the Tailors and Skinners in 1563 (confirmed in the next year), to the Glovers in 1564 and to the Shearmen in 1566. The Drapers had also figured

[1] Gross, II. 1, 2, 55, 89, 186—7, 208, 250.

in the Statute Book on two occasions. The Acts
8 Elizabeth, c. 7, and 14 Elizabeth, c. 12, had both
been concerned with the affairs of the Drapers of
Shrewsbury in their capacity of state agents for the
regulation of industry[1].

In 1605 the company of Drapers was incorporated
by James I. and the Smiths in 1621. The Tailors
received a composition in 1627 and another in 1686.
The Tanners were regulated by a new composition
in 1639, the Smiths in 1661, the Barbers in 1662.
The records of the Mercers contain entries of
"cessments for renewing the Composition" in several
years—1639, 1640, 1644, 1646 etc.

Many new Gilds formed. In many places of recent growth, or where the
old Gilds had been destroyed without there having
been any construction of fresh machinery to take
their place, deliberate grants were made of new
trade companies. The Merchant Adventurers of
Exeter were incorporated by Elizabeth expressly for
the purpose of supervising trade and "on account of
the inconveniences arising from the excessive number
of artificers and unskilled persons occupying the art
or mystery of merchandising[2]." The charter which
was granted "hominibus mistere Marceriorum" at
York in 1581 allowed them to form themselves into
a company under officers chosen with the consent of
the municipal authorities: the evils which necessi-

[1] Cf. infra, pp. 90—91. The repealing statute (14 Eliz. c. 12)
avowed that not only had the former Act been "supposed for the
benefit of the said town" but had also been intended for the
"advancing of the Corporation of Drapers, Cottoners and Friezers
of the said town."

[2] Gross, II. 87.

tated the forming of the company being expressly
stated to be such as had ensued from a lack of due
regulation of trade[1]. At Axbridge every house-
holder, whether engaged in trade or not, was ordered,
in 1614, to enrol himself in one of the three companies of the town[2].

In all these charters care was taken that the *Intimate*
new corporations should be in due subordination to *connection with civic*
the town authorities[3]. In some places the Mayor *authori-*
or other officer of the town was *ex officio* head of *ties.*
the Gild. Sometimes it was granted to the " Mayor,
bailiffs and commonalty and their successors for ever,
that they shall and may from time to time ordain,
create, and establish, a society, gild, or fraternity, of
one master and wardens of every art, mystery and
occupation used or occupied, or hereafter to be used
or occupied, within the said city and the suburbs
thereof; and that they with the assistance of the
wardens of the said arts and mysteries may make,
constitute, ordain and establish laws, constitutions
and ordinances for the public utility and profit and
for the better rule and regiment of our city of
Winchester and of the mysteries of the citizens
and inhabitants of the same[4]." Such power of
supervision was generally allowed to the municipal
authorities. The head of the Gild frequently took
his oath of office before the Mayor. The Common

---

[1] Gross, II. 281.   Cf. also pp. 12, 87, 199, 234, 247—8, 250,
281, 355, 360.

[2] *Ibid.*, 12.

[3] *Ibid.*, 56, 90, 91, 176, 186, 193, 199, 234, 247, 251, 264, 364,
385.

[4] Merewether and Stephens, 1408.

Council of the town had power to make such ordinances as it might think fit for the good estate, order and rule of the Gildsmen. In certain cases too the Mayor had power "to call and admitt unto the same Free Guild and Burgeshipp of the said Town such and soe many able and discreete persons as...shall seeme fitt" and also "uppon any iust and lawful grounds and causes to disffranchise them[1].' Under these conditions the public authorities of the town would be ready to support the companies. In some cases they were expressly ordered to do so. At Shrewsbury we shall find the town Bailiffs assisting the companies in the efforts of the latter to prevent the encroachments of foreigners.

What all this change and reform amounted to was this. The system of Gilds was re-organised and strengthened. Part of the functions which the Craft Gilds had performed were taken over by the state. Part were left to be still performed by the companies. The companies were in all cases brought into the closest possible connection with the town and the town authorities.

As regards the designation of these 16th century trade associations it appears that they were generally termed societies or companies in public documents, probably because the name "Gild" might seem to savour somewhat of the Chantries and mass-priests. But in their own books and lists they still called themselves Gilds and fraternities.

The new companies show per- Though they differed essentially from these, as has been already pointed out, yet, viewed super-

[1] Cromwell's Charter to Swansea. Gross, II. 234.

ficially, they might seem to have retained many of *manence of*
the features of the old Gilds.   In practice they bore *Gild-*
feeling.
no small share of the burden of public charities.
They were also not unmindful of the wants of their
members, though of course these now consisted of
masters only.   Elizabeth's charter to the Merchant
Adventurers of Bristol ordered them to distribute
yearly among twenty poor men twenty "vestes pan-
neas" and to assist all of the company who were impoverished by mischance or otherwise.

In their ordinances and compositions they were
even more similar in appearance to the old Gilds.
The composition which Elizabeth granted to the
Glovers of Shrewsbury in 1564 is as strict as any
mediæval regulation.   It restricted all masters to a
maximum of three apprentices.   It confined each
brother to a single shop, and to the selling of the
products of his own work only.   It authorised the
Wardens to seize corrupt or insufficient wares, and
was altogether a most thorough piece of industrial
regulation, entirely modelled on the lines of the old
Gild arrangements.

Other indications of the same spirit were not
lacking.   In 1621 "by and with the allowance and
agreement of the right worthie" the town authorities,
skins and fells were ordered to be purchased only
between sunrise and sunset.   As though the Wardens
of the Barbers' company had not been sufficiently
thorough in executing their duties the new composition which the company received from Charles
II. in 1662 made provision for the appointment of a
searcher and defined the duties appertaining to the

office. The composition granted to the Smiths in
1621 forbade the keeping of two shops by a single
tradesman in the town, and disallowed the employment of foreigners for a longer period than a week
without express permission obtained from the Wardens. The composition of the Tailors, granted in
1627, forbade the wearing of "any lyvere of any
Earle Lorde Barronett Knight Esquire or Gentleman" while occupying any Gild office; prohibited
unfair competition and the employment of foreigners;
and ordered that "noe pettie Chapman or other p'son
or p'sons shall buy any Skynnes of furre" within
the town. In the composition of 1686 the articles
are repeated against indiscriminate admittance of
foreigners, and against the piratical infringement of
unfree persons on the province of the brethren.

The "Regulated Companies" which arose about
the same time were a further development of the
same movement, but on a larger scale. In many
respects indeed the Craft Gilds of the 14th and
15th centuries were but little different from the
Regulated Companies of the 17th. Admission was
practically free on payment of a fine, the individual
so received into membership being left to prosecute
his trade in his own way, by his own means, and to
his own particular profit.

Though altered conditions of trade make their work difficult. But the difficulties attendant on attempts to
regulate expanding trade were daily growing greater
and more numerous. "The false making and short
lengths of all sortes of cloths and stuffes" necessitated the appointment by the Mercers of two men
"to oversee and look after" these things in 1638.

The Barbers too in 1662 empowered the stewards to search for bad materials. In 1639 the Glovers' company was brought to something like a crisis "by the taking of many apprentices." It was thought necessary to dock each brother of one of the apprentices allowed by the Elizabethan composition of 1564[1].

The frequency with which it was necessary to renew the compositions, the reiteration of the same articles,—against employing foreigners, against unfair competition, against neglect of the legal period of apprenticeship,—again shows the futility of such restrictions. Actions against intruders even thus early figure frequently on the records. In those of the Tailors and Skinners the decision of the company under date of August 23, 1627, is recorded thus :—" The Wardens and Sitters met and agreed that the Wardens should fetch process for Intruders and implead them before the Council in the Marches, and Mr Chelmicke to draw the bill against them."

The history of the Welsh woollen trade in its connection with Shrewsbury well exhibits the economic policy of the day, and as it therefore illustrates several of the points with which we have been concerned it may be given here at some length.

In the earlier part of the 16th century Oswestry *The features of the period seen in* appears to have been the principal market for the Welsh products. At Shrewsbury however there was

---

[1] Cf. the ordinance which appears in the Tailors' records, A.D. 1711, April 11. "No combrother shall at any one time have more "than two apprentices, one having served 3½ years before the "other apprentice be bound, and no apprentice above 17 years "taken, and he must be unmarried."

history of Welsh woollen trade of Shrewsbury. also a large woollen trade, as we learn from the Act 8 Elizabeth, cap. 7, entitled, " An Act touching the Drapers, Cottoners, and Frizers of Shrewsbury." This statute recited that there had been time out of mind a Gild of the art and mystery of Drapers legally incorporated in Shrewsbury, which had *Flourish-ing in reign of Elizabeth,* usually set on work above six hundred persons of the art or science of Shearmen or Frizers. Of late however it had come to pass that divers persons, not being members of the said company, neither brought up in the use of the said trade, had "with great disorder, upon a mere covetous desire and mind, intromitted with and occupied the said trade of buying Welsh cloth or lining, having no knowledge, experience or skill in the same." The result is asserted to be that the men of the company are impoverished and like to be brought to ruin unless speedy remedy be provided. It is therefore for-bidden that anyone inhabiting Shrewsbury shall " occupy the trade" of buying Welsh woollens, unless he be free of the company of the Drapers[1].

but injured by over-regula-tion Such a stringent regulation of trade met with directly contrary results to those which had been expected. A statute six years later acknowledges the failure of the measure, although it attempts to shift the blame from the shoulders of the Govern-ment by representing the measure as one taken at *caused by selfish interests.* the request of the Drapers, instead of as a piece of state-craft[2].

[1] It was also directed against the paying of the Shearmen in kind.
[2] Cf. also 18 Eliz. cap. 15 (Goldsmiths) : 8 Eliz. cap. 11 (Haberdashers).

The statute of 14 Elizabeth, cap. 12, almost
entirely repeals 8 Elizabeth, cap. 7, " at the humble
suit of the inhabitants of the said town and also of
the said artificers, for whose benefit the said Act was
supposed to be provided[1]....For experience hath
plainly taught in the said town that the said Act
hath not only not brought the good effect that then
was hoped and surmised, but also hath been and now
is like to be the very greatest cause of the im-
poverishing and undoing of the poor Artificers and
others at whose suit the said Act was procured, for
that there be now, sithence the making of the said
Act, much fewer persons to set them awork than
afore."

The whole incident is extremely interesting.   It
affords an excellent illustration of the way in which
the Gilds were in some places made state agents for
carrying into effect 5 Elizabeth, cap. 14.   It also shows
plainly that state intervention was beginning to be
found harmful even by the men of that day.   It
evidences, moreover, how large the Welsh trade of
Shrewsbury had already grown.

Oswestry however continued to be the chief
emporium, and the Drapers of Shrewsbury repaired
thither every Monday for a long period after the
date of the statutes we have been considering.

The company of the Drapers was the most con- *The*
siderable and influential of the trade associations of *Drapers'*
Shrewsbury.   It numbered among its brethren the *repre-*
great majority of the chief burgesses of the town.   Its *interests*

Company

sents the

---

[1] In 1570—1 when Sir Henry Sidney, Lord President of Wales,
passed through Shrewsbury.

of Shrews-
bury relations with the municipal corporation were, as
would be expected, very intimate. It was the
custom of the Drapers to attend divine worship in
the church of St Alkmund before setting out for the
Oswestry market. In 1614 an order was made for
the payment of six and eightpence to the clerk of the
church for ringing the morning bell to prayers on
Monday mornings at six o'clock, not by the company
as we should expect, but by the corporation[1].

in oppo-   There arose considerable competition for the
sition to
Oswestry, lucrative market which the expansion of Welsh
industry was every day rendering more profitable.
Chester, The inhabitants of Chester made a vigorous attempt
to obtain the erection in their city of "a staple for
the cottons and friezes of North Wales." Shrewsbury was however enabled to prevent the completion
of the scheme[2].

London ;   The attempt of London to obtain a share in the
trade seemed fraught with so much danger that the
two rivals, Shrewsbury and Oswestry, made common
cause against the intruder. The complaint was a
general one that the merchants of London and their
factors forestalled and engrossed productions before
especially they came to market. These obnoxious practices
the last. seem to have been carried to a particularly dis-
tasteful length on the borders of Wales. The
transactions of a London dealer named Thomas
Davies in 1619 appear to have brought matters to a
crisis.

There had been complaints about the same man,

---

[1] Shrewsbury Corporation Records.
[2] State Papers, Domestic, 1566? (p. 285).

with others, previously. He had, by craft, obtained
admission to the freedom of Oswestry, by which
means he could the better purchase the Welsh
cloths. These he then carried to London where he
sold them "privately"[1]—that is, not in the proper
and public market. The Drapers of the two towns
petitioned that the matter might be settled before
the Council[2]. Being foiled in his attempt to plead
his freedom of Oswestry[2] Davies appealed to the
Lord Mayor and Corporation of the Metropolis to
support his claims to trade throughout England in
right of his citizenship of London[3]. The order of
the Council depriving the Londoners of what they
called their "ancient privilege" evoked strenuous
opposition in the Metropolis, and petitions nume-
rously signed[4] were sent in asserting that the
Drapers of Shrewsbury and Oswestry had obtained
the order by misrepresentation[5]. It does not appear
that these petitions were successful, as Thomas
Davies in his examination before the Council a little
later, expressed his willingness to resign his London
freedom and to confine his dealings to Oswestry.
The fear of creating a precedent which would be
largely followed, and with probable detriment to the
trade of Shrewsbury and Oswestry, restrained the
Council from allowing him to do this[6].

Not that the trade of Shrewsbury, at any rate,

[1] State Papers, Domestic, 1619, Oct.?   [2] Ibid., 1620, Jan.?

[3] Ibid., 1620, Jan.? (There are several petitions against other
intruders also, by the countenance of the City of London, "who
wish to engross all markets.")

[4] Ibid., 1620, Jan.?   [5] Ibid., 1620, Jan. 28.

[6] Ibid., 1620, Feb. 21.

was likely to decrease through any apathy on the part of its company of Drapers. They were on the contrary singularly active at this time. And there was every need for them to be vigilant. For, with the object of stimulating the industry of the Principality by allowing a more extensive market, and probably also as a result of the recent proceedings between the Drapers of Shrewsbury and Oswestry and the citizens of London, a Proclamation was issued allowing free trade in Welsh cloths. The novelty pleased neither the Welshmen[1] nor the merchants of the borders. To the latter the chief consequence seemed to be that the French company, which had the monopoly of exporting such goods to France, was enabled to purchase direct from the manufacturers in Wales instead of through the Drapers. The case was undoubtedly a hard one for the latter, who could not export. Consequently their grievance was a real one, and, as they showed in their petition to the Council, ruin stared them in the face unless they too might be allowed to export and so dispose of the large stock which was thrown on their hands[2].

But at the same time they were successfully endeavouring to draw the Welsh trade from Oswestry entirely to Shrewsbury[3].

[1] State Papers, Domestic, 1622. Several petitions from North Wales against the Proclamation.

[2] *Ibid.*, 1621. Petition of Drapers of Shrewsbury.

[3] *Ibid.*, 1621, May 21. Petition of Clothiers of North Wales: the Drapers of Shrewsbury are trying to draw all trade to Shrewsbury, which will be their ruin.

They had prepared for the attempt by obtaining a new charter from Elizabeth's successor in 1605. That they had lost no time in putting their privileges to practical use is seen from their answer, four years later, to a mandate issued to them by Thomas Howard, Earl of Suffolk, who held the overlordship of Oswestry, to desist from their efforts to undermine the trade of his town. Their answer is entitled " The Copy of a Letter sent by the Company to the Earle of Suffolk, Lord Chamberlen of his Majesties Househoulde, the 24 June 1609," and begins

> " Right Honerabell,
> " Your letter bearing date the second of
> " this June by the hands of Mr Kinaston wee
> " have receaved : wherein ytt appeareth yor
> " Lordship was informed that wee the Societie
> " of Drapers wentt abowte by underarte and
> " menesses to withdrawe your markett of
> " Walshe Clothe from your towne of Oswester."

Though they proceed to exculpate themselves from the charge, it is evident their intention was to pursue in the future the same policy which they had hitherto practised. In 1618 Suffolk fell and *All competitors worsted.* Oswestry was deprived of his support, so that in 1621 the Shrewsbury Drapers felt justified in resolving " That they will not buy Cloth at Oswestry or elsewhere than Salop," in spite of the opposition of the clothiers of North Wales[1], who, whether from convenience or old association, appeared to prefer

---

[1] State Papers, Domestic; Oswestry Corporation Records, printed in *S. A. S.* Vol. III.

Oswestry as the locale of their market. However the Drapers' company, assisted by the town[1], was sufficiently powerful to turn the Proclamation allowing free trade in Welsh cloths to their own good, and the market was drawn to Shrewsbury in spite of orders by the Council that it should be re-established at Oswestry. The company did not hesitate to declare to the Council itself that they were prepared, if necessary, to disregard its orders. By 1633 the market at Oswestry had practically died out. It was held at Shrewsbury on Wednesdays, and afterwards on Fridays. In 1649 the date was altered to Thursday.

To the Market House flocked the Welsh farmers, their bales of cloth being borne to the town on the backs of hardy ponies. The merchandise was exposed for sale in the large room upstairs. The Drapers assembled beneath, and proceeded to make their purchases in order of seniority, according to ancient usage. The custom which the Welshmen brought to the town easily accounts for the keenness *Expansion* of the competition to secure the market. For a long *of trade,* time the trade flourished. Gradually however the *and inter-* action of "foreigners" in buying from the Welsh *lopers,* manufacturers at their homes[2] broke down the monopoly which Shrewsbury had so long enjoyed. At the end of the 18th century the sales had

[1] In 1622 the Bailiffs had requested a loan from the Mercers towards the establishing of a market for Welsh cloth in Shrewsbury.

[2] The traders of Liverpool seem to have been the first to do this, so far as the Welsh trade of Shrewsbury was concerned. Cf. Owen's *Shrewsbury.*

shrunk to miserable proportions.   In 1803 the room
over the market was relinquished by the Drapers,
and though a certain amount of Welsh trade was
still carried on, it withdrew gradually from the town
until it finally left Shrewsbury altogether.   The *destroy*
Drapers might have realised that the time for re- *Shrews-*
stricting trade to the freemen of their company was *monopoly.*
past.

CHAPTER VI.

THE DEGENERACY OF THE COMPANIES.

Outside competition

THE competition of "interlopers" ruined the Welsh trade of Shrewsbury. It was not, as we have seen, from any lack of vigilance on the part of the companies. Stimulated by their new compositions they became extremely active. As early as 1622 the actions against "foreigners" begin. Soon afterwards they become of frequent occurrence until at length the books of the companies are almost mere records of a daily struggle for existence.

inevitable under the altered conditions of trade.

This was of course inevitable under the altered conditions of trade. But the companies exhibited in themselves all the radical defects which must pertain to such a system when it has outgrown its necessity. We have seen how free the earlier companies were from friction with the municipal authorities. In the 17th century this is changed. The propriety of setting up a May-pole had formerly been almost the only ground of conflict between the bailiffs and the craftsmen. But in 1639 we find that the Tanners were thought to be overstepping their powers; the corporation appointed a committee to examine their composition. Some seven-

But the companies themselves are unsatisfactory.

teen years later, extreme measures had to be taken *Friction with the town authorities;* with regard to the same company. It was the custom for the charters to be inspected by the corporation periodically. In 1656 the Tanners refused to comply with the request to produce their composition for the mayor's perusal, with the result that the company was prosecuted by the corporation[1].

The town had been willing to support the Drapers in their measures to draw the Welsh trade to Shrewsbury, but it did not approve of the line of action they tried subsequently to take, namely, to limit all the trade to their own members. In 1653 regulations were framed to prevent the company "forestalling or engrossing the Welsh Flannels, Cloaths etc.[2]" A more serious abuse transpired in connection with the Feltmakers' company in 1667. They refused to make one who had been lawfully apprenticed to the trade in Shrewsbury free of their company. On this occasion the mayor and aldermen exercised their right of supervision by ordering the Wardens to admit the man, "and the Mayor is desired to give him the oath of a Freeman of the said Company[3]." The importance of the mayor being thus empowered by the municipal authorities to administer the oath of admittance to one of the Gilds is very great, and shows how real was the subordination of the latter to the town when the corporation chose to exert its rights.

[1] Orders of Corporation (collected by Godolphin Edwardes, Mayor in 1729). *S. A. S.* Vol. xi.
[2] *Ibid.*   [3] *Ibid.*

An order of the corporation[1] directing that
burgesses only are to be elected Wardens of the
companies points to another abuse, the existence of
which is proved by other evidence, viz., the admittance of non-residents in the town to membership
in the companies on payment of a sufficiently large
entrance fee. Yet the extent to which corruption
could go was seen forty years later when the corporation stultified itself by passing an order[2] allowing
the Haberdashers to elect persons, though they
might not be burgesses, as Wardens of their company.

The general impression which such transactions
leave is that extreme laxity prevailed in all departments. The town woke up for a moment in 1702
when the prospect perhaps of a harvest of unpaid
fines induced them to make an effort to recover all
such[3]. It is to be regretted that nothing remains to
show to what extent the abuse had prevailed, nor
how far the present effort was successful. The
annual fine of the Bakers' company was £3. 6s. 8d.
which they appear to have generally paid with
considerable reluctance[4]. The supply of provision
to the town seems to have given much trouble in
the early years of the eighteenth century. Permission was given, in 1730, to the country butchers
to sell in the town unless the town butchers could

[1] Orders of Corporation (1689).

[2] *Ibid.* (1729).   [3] *Ibid.*

[4] "1619. That the Corporation endeavour to compel the
wardens of the Bakers' Company to pay their old annuity of
£4. 6s. 8d. (sic) to the Corporation." Orders of Corporation
printed in Phillips' *History of Shrewsbury*, p. 170.

furnish meat in sufficient quantity. Similar permission was accorded to the country bakers, if the
Bakers' company in the town would not pay their
yearly fine. This they were unwilling, or unable,
to do, and the country bakers were in consequence
called in[1].

The picture given by such incidents is not more
significant of the degeneracy of the Gilds than is
that which the friction of the companies one with *with one*
another presents. The Mercers and the Drapers *another,*
had frequently made mutual complaints of intrusion:
the Mercers and the Glovers also appear as great
rivals in later years. In 1679 and at several subsequent dates there were actions at law between
the two companies. In 1727 the records of the
Glovers show that similar actions were again in
process. In 1721 the company unanimously agreed
to withstand the Tailors in the matter of widow
Steen, whom they pledge themselves to support;
"and that shee may goe on with makeing Brichess
peruided shee dos not line them with flonen or
Buckrom or cennet onlye Lether."

Nor is the evidence of intestine friction within *and with*
the Gilds themselves less significant of decay. So *their own*
early as 1636 the Mercers were fain to confess that *members.*
the spirit of mutual assistance had disappeared, in
the order which they passed to the effect that any
combrother refusing to pay his assessment was to be
distrained upon by authority of the Wardens. There
are several records of such distraints. In 1700 they

[1] Orders of Corporation printed in Phillips' *History of Shrewsbury.*

find it necessary to pass an ordinance against freemen taking the sons of intruders as apprentices.
The records of the other companies are, similarly,
full of like evidences of demoralisation. The companies are declared to be impoverished by the
taking of inordinate numbers of apprentices. The
same sort of abuse is found in a complaint which
appears in the Glovers' books in 1656: "the company is much impoverished by the taking in of
foreigners freemen such as have not served" their
due apprenticeship. "The disorderly manner of
electing Wardens" about which the Glovers have
to "take account" in 1668 points to a great de-
terioration in the manner of holding Gild meetings
from that which has been sketched in a previous
chapter[1]. Worse than all is the confession that the
Gild brothers have sunk so low as to connive at
intruders "for fraudulent lucre and gain[2]." The
Saddlers have the same sort of complaint in 1740.
Some brethren are infringing on the trades of others:
resolutions are passed against such conduct. Their
books show that the resolutions were soon forgotten[3].
The other Gilds experienced similar difficulties. In
1745 the Barbers levied a fine of ten shillings on
brethren who should so far forget themselves as to
instruct "men or women servants to dress hair."

The problem of regulating trade would have been

---

[1] Cf. supra, p. 44.

[2] Glovers' records, 1681.

[3] 1782. Two members were called upon to show cause why
they practise a profession contrary to that they have sworn to
follow.

difficult enough under the most favourable circumstances. With the Gilds in the condition which we
have been considering it was an impossibility. There
was indeed a feature in the modern companies which
at the outset deprived the attempt to utilise them
beneficially for trade-purposes of all chance of
success.

The old Gilds, which had lived through the *The Gilds*
shocks of the Reformation, and the Elizabethan *have changed*
changes, had quite altered their character. The
new ones which had arisen differed widely from the
old fraternities. Instead of being brotherhoods of
craftsmen desirous of advancing the public weal,
they were now mere societies of capitalists, intent *to capi-*
only on private and personal advantage. As a *talist com-panies.*
writer of 1680 observes "most of our ancient Corporations and Guilds [have] become oppressive
Oligarchies[1]." There is a constant endeavour to
restrict the companies to favoured individuals.
Every "foreigner" is subjected to a heavy fine,
which grows larger in amount as the companies
feel the trade slipping from their hands in spite of
their desperate endeavours to restrict it. The new
compositions continually point to this abuse by
bringing back the fines to their original sum, or
rather reducing them to an amount less inordinate
than that which they have irregularly reached.
The admission stamp of the Saddlers was 4/- in
1784. It reached 8/2 in 1799. In 1831 it was
20/2. The Mercers' fine was fixed at £40. 6s. 8d. in
1789, "besides fees." In 1823 it had sunk to £20.

---

[1] *Britannia Languens*, p. 355.

The Mercers were of course one of the richest of the companies, yet the sum was a large one to pay for the privilege of opening a shop in a provincial town.

Other means to restrict themselves were also attempted. Increase in the number of apprentices was viewed with disfavour. There are frequent complaints of the "impoverishment" of the companies through the indiscriminate admittance of "foreigners." All the evidence shows how entirely they have degenerated into mere societies of capitalists. Their records almost decline into bald columns of pounds, shillings and pence. For it was to this completeness of degradation that the social body had sunk. The merest selfishness was lauded as a patriotic virtue. Private gain was recommended as a public benefit. Social disintegration and industrial anarchy ruled supreme, and when commercial success had come to be looked upon as the one avenue to honour and advancement, it was not to be expected that the companies would escape the general infection. They formed simply one among many means by which the individual was enabled to fill his own pockets at the cost of a suffering and squalid populace.

This change in their character, which became more marked as time went by, naturally was not unattended by a change in their government. All authority became engrossed by the richer members. The Four Assistants with the Wardens and Stewards formed a close aristocratic board. Brentano, speaking it would appear more particularly of the London companies, says[1] the king nominated the first members of this court and afterwards as vacancies occurred they were filled by co-optation. This was not exactly the case with the Shrewsbury companies. There the annual meeting[2] retained a considerable power in the election of officers to the last. In some cases the Assistants or Four Men were elected freely by the assembled combrethren, in others two only were thus elected, the two retiring Wardens completing the number. The Tailors' composition of 1563 provided that the two Wardens should be elected by the whole Gild: the Four Assistants were then nominated by these Wardens "for advising them in the Government of the Gild." The Wardens and Assistants then proceeded to nominate the two Stewards.

They were thus as exclusive and aristocratic as the town corporations had become. The degeneracy of the latter had been largely intensified by the degeneracy of the former. For the principal members of the companies were the principal members of the town corporation, which had silently, since the fourteenth century, been usurping the ancient powers of the general body of the burgesses. It was the companies which mainly profited by it. They profited indirectly, by the influence which they exercised through individual members on the town council, which had obtained part of the functions of the Leet. They profited directly as they themselves acquired definitely other of the powers of the Court Leet. They

The companies and the close corporations.

---

[1] p. 88.

[2] Consisting however of masters only.

became the chief or the sole medium for the acquisition of municipal freedom, and were distinct town organs for the regulation of trade and industry.

It is by reason of the widely-reaching influence of their degeneracy that their later history is of importance. For as regards the poorer members of society their history is useless. The workman dis-

The jour-
neymen no
longer in
the com-
panies.

appears from their books. That he no longer was looked upon as the brother member of the masters is quite evident.

" Our workmen do work hard, but we live at ease,
" We go when we will, and we come when we please[1]."

They begin
to form
benefit
societies,

The most general means which the poor adopted to help themselves was the formation of Friendly Societies. These arose in great numbers during the 18th century. The companies were not slow in helping to swell public subscriptions and in assisting to pauperise the labouring class. To the necessity of rendering real help to their unfortunate workmen they were however entirely oblivious. This side of the work performed by the old Gilds had been almost wholly overlooked by the post-reformation companies, though it had been one of the most important of their predecessors' functions. It was found that society could not get along without something of the kind, and as the higher companies would not perform the work, the lower craftsmen found it necessary to do it themselves. Here was a distinct severance of interest between employers and workmen, yet it does not seem unlikely that it was

[1] Macaulay, *History of England*, Vol. I. p. 204, n.

the old Gilds themselves which formed the models
for the new societies. At any rate the analogies *animated*
between the Gilds and the Benefit Societies, in the *by much of the old*
earlier phases of the latter, and looking at the social *Gild-*
and religious side of the former, are very striking[1]. *spirit.*
The simple rules of trade association show as much
concern for the morals of members as did the
charters of the Gilds: they had their annual feast,
provided by subscription: they usually went in their
procession to the parish church on the day of the
feast. They were perhaps the earliest signs of that
necessary return to something like the old Gild
system which the later Trades Unions have done
so much to bring about. The companies watched
them grow up without a twinge of conscience, though
it was their own neglect of duty which made such
associations an absolute necessity. Being the only
forms of combination which were left unmolested by
the government they were extensively formed, and
this was well, for the need of them was very great.

In spite of unmistakeable signs of inevitable *Difficulties*
changes the companies refused to take warning. *of reform;*
Their reform was indeed difficult, and, as it proved, *members*
impossible. The workmen as we have seen could *would not,*
not, the masters would not, take steps in this direc- *state*
tion. The state derived too good an income from *would not,*
them to be anxious for a change. The admission
stamps, constantly increasing in amount, were a
profitable source of revenue. The notices of "cessments for renewing the composition" are frequent.

[1] Cf. Howell, *Conflicts of Capital and Labour*, pp. 16, 62, 79,
103, 109, 472.

There were also continual contributions of men and money for the "exigencies of the State[1]." In 1798 the Mercers voted £100 annually to the government "during the continuance of the war." The town *the town* also seemed to profit by them. They were obliged, *authorities* some of them at all events, to exhibit their composi- *would not.* tions annually or periodically to the mayor and pay a customary fine on doing so. They continued to be of some service to the community in the inefficient condition of the public police. Their social utility to the town was also in their favour. In 1608 the corporation provided materials in case of fire, when each of the companies was required to maintain its proper proportion of hooks and buckets. Entries relating to the "spout or water engine" are frequent in their records. In aid of procuring public benefits the companies were not backward. Their chests were readily opened to assist towards improvements in the town, such as widening of streets, erection of bridges and the like.

To the last also they preserved something of their charitable character, though its exercise was as open to criticism as other forms of poor relief during the eighteenth century. Nevertheless if the membership lists of the Drapers and the Mercers could be made public they would be found to contain the majority of the public benefactors of Shrewsbury during this period. Public charities, such as the Infirmary and the Lancaster School received annual subscriptions until the companies came to an end.

---

[1] Resolution of Saddlers in 1798, voting £50.

The necessity of continuing the annuities to the inmates of S. Chad's almshouses formed a chief argument against the dissolution of the Mercers' company. "The Worshipful Company of Drapers" still subscribes to schools and charities year by year.

In these circumstances we cannot wonder that the old companies found many champions. The following letter is valuable as affording a view of the contemporaneous opinion held of the Gilds by a man of ordinary common sense and average education. It appeared in the *Salopian Journal* of August 27, 1823. It was evoked by a decision of the Judges of Assize in favour of the Mercers' company in an important case to which reference will be made in a later page. It was addressed to the editor of the newspaper and commenced— *Contemporaneous opinion of the companies.*

"SIR,

As the Company commonly called 'the United Company of Mercers, Grocers, Ironmongers, and Goldsmiths' in this town have established the validity of their ancient customs by a suit at law of which there is no account of their having done so since the time when the King's Court for the Marches of Wales was held at Ludlow; at which time and place the Council then, who held the pleas, determined also a like suit in their favour: and as there is much argument for and against the existence and usage of this incorporate body; permit me to lay before the public an outline of both, that the subject at least might be better understood than we often hear it repeated. It is contended against, as exercising an arbitrary monopoly of trade, to the detriment and oppression of the subjects of the realm; and which is moreover injurious to the town itself, by depriving the Trade thereof of that competition which brings down the Articles of manufacture to a fair marketable value for the supply of its inhabitants. These are the charges against them, which if indeed they could be substantiated would be sufficient to show that their existence was an evil. But let us look at the facts on the other side of the question, and see whether there is any reality in these serious charges. In the first place the Companies hold it requisite, in order to be free of their body, that all but the sons of Freemen shall serve a regular apprenticeship to one of the Corporation. Now in this they have been sanctioned and dictated to by the ancient law of the land... that youths might be properly taught their respective arts, and that the community might not be imposed upon by pretenders to that which they were not properly acquainted with.

On Foreigners or such as have not served a regular apprenticeship they impose a fine of £20, before they will admit them as freemen, and certainly in doing this they do not over-rate a seven years' servitude, when the one is made equivalent to the other.

Let us now see to the application of the money. A fund is made of it, somewhat similar to 'Benefit Societies.' No part of it is applied to private purposes; for even the Company's annual feast, about which there is so much said, is not always at the expense of the fund, but [is] borne individually; and the utility of such a feast to promote harmony and goodwill, is acknowledged by all Societies[1]. But further, these funds are confined

---

[1] This sentiment finds expression even in some of the compositions.

to the relief of decayed and deserving members of the
Companies[1], and to every charitable and public emer-
gency wherein the general interest or welfare of the
town is concerned; and their annual disbursements, for
centuries past, have been regularly serviceable to the
community at large as well as to individual cases of
distress. This the account of their expenditure will
show. Now, then this monopoly, as it is called, extends
no further than to exact an apprenticeship of seven
years, or to a fine of £20; the former sanctioned by law
and the latter a sum of no comparative amount to a
respectable person, desirous of establishing a respectable trade, especially if there be any truth in the
argument, that goods are sold by this corporate body for
more money than they would be, if no such corporation
existed. Neither can the fine be called excessive, because it is added to a stock which he from whom it is
exacted directs in common to be applied to the common
good; and which he may himself, as many others have
done in cases of distress, receive back again with large
additions.

But the increased population of Birmingham and
Manchester is brought forward as a proof of towns
flourishing where trade is what is called *free*. Let us
look a little into this argument. Are not the wares
vended in these places proverbially *bad*? Do not all
manner of imposters from these places deluge the country
with their spurious goods, and impose them upon the
unwary part of the public? Are these towns to be
compared with London, Liverpool, Bristol, for respect-
ability of their trade, for the goodness and cheapness
of their articles, when the quality is taken into account?

---

[1] That is, masters only, not workmen.

Yet the trade of these latter towns is regulated by corporations.

I contend therefore that the Corporation in question is *beneficial* to this town and county, inasmuch as it tends to protect it from the inundations of empirics and imposters, while it holds out no hindrance to the fair and honest dealer who has a mind to compete with its respectable tradesmen and settle amongst them. I am not in trade myself; but hope I shall always see my native town preserved from that sort of population which it has never yet been disgraced with.

I have the honour to be, Mr Editor,

In technical language,

A COMBROTHER OF THE GUILD.

SHREWSBURY, Aug. 22, 1823."

CHAPTER VII.

SHREWSBURY SHOW.

A STRANGE glamour hangs around the Middle *Character-*
Ages. We know so little of man's actual life in *istic features*
those years,—and what little we do know seems to *of the*
partake so largely of the mysterious and the pic- *Middle Ages.*
turesque,—all his modes of life and manners of
thought are so far removed from our own,—that
mediæval history would easily resolve itself into an
enchanting pageant bright with its colour and be-
wildering with its contradictions. It is perhaps in
the strange contrasts which are presented to us
that its chief wonder is found. In those years we
find lust and rapine, and sacrilege and tyranny, side
by side with the fairest forms of chivalry[1], the most
devoted readiness to champion the cause of religion,
the firmest attachment to the forms of law[2]. We see
only the prominent lights and the great shadows
of the picture, but all that should go to make it
human and comprehensible to us is hidden under
the dust of centuries.

[1] *The Happy Warrior* of Wordsworth gives us probably a very
true idea of the mediæval conception of the perfect knight.

[2] Cf. Stubbs' *Lectures on Constitutional History.*

We have noticed the existence of something of this contradictory spirit in the view we have had of the early Gilds[1]. The elevated ideal which they set before their members must of course have been far above the level which was ever actually reached. We may smile at their vain attempts after the impossible, yet we cannot but allow that their perseverance betokens the widespread acceptance of a nobler conception of human life than is common in our own too merely practical age. To the men of those days there seemed no great incongruity in the lofty ideals of the Gild-compositions and the lower standard which the brethren actually attained. It added but another to the many striking contrasts which environed their daily life.

Fondness for pageantry. That life was one passed largely in dulness and perhaps comparative squalor. But the occasions of colour and merriment were not few. Each season had its festivities, social and religious, when rich and poor met on something like equal ground in the *Its social importance.* rude merry-making. This feature in ordinary life was not without its social importance, and if only for this reason no account of the Gilds would be complete which failed to take notice of their processions and, in so doing, of the general life and habits of the brethren at the different epochs of Gild history. We have now nothing to take the place of those occasions of mutual enjoyment and mirth, when "ceremony doff'd his pride" without censure, when the bashful apprentice might perhaps tread a measure with his master's daughter, and

[1] Cf. supra, p. 47.

when the condescending mistress of the house might
even allow herself to be led out for a dance by one
or other of her goodman's journeymen.

"A Christmas gambol oft would cheer
"A poor man's heart through half the year[1]."

We have already seen how important an influence *The*
religious feelings had in the actions of the Gilds. *Corpus
Christi*
Among the yearly festivals the feast of Corpus *procession.*
Christi soon became one of the most splendid for
pomp and pageantry, and to it the Gilds were
naturally attracted. Some indeed existed with the
primary object of ensuring the glory of this particular feast. Most important of these was the Corpus
Christi Gild at York[2]. The Gild of the Holy Trinity,
also at York, concerned itself with the annual production of a religious play illustrating the Lord's
Prayer. The Gilds of S. Helen (which represented
the Invention of the Cross), of S. Mary, and of
Corpus Christi, at Beverley[3], were other famous
fraternities with similar objects. At Stamford was
one which maintained a secular play[4]. In most
towns in England it became the custom for the
Gilds, each with its banners and insignia, to accompany the Corpus Christi procession: in some places
the event seems to have become especially pictu-
resque. At Coventry[5] and also at Shrewsbury, the

[1] Scott's *Marmion.*
[2] Brentano, p. 21.   [3] *Ibid.* p. 21.
[4] Toulmin Smith, p. 192.
[5] It is a curious coincidence that these two towns which
earlier evinced such jealousy towards one another's procession (cf.
supra, p. 63) should have maintained it longest.

procession has lasted in some sort down to our own day[1]. At the former city Lady Godiva has even lately ridden, though at fitful and uncertain intervals: at the latter town, although the procession has now become a thing of the past, it is little more than a decade since "Shrewsbury Show" was to be seen annually, on the Monday following the feast of Corpus Christi, passing along under the eaves of the timbered houses of the old border town.

The prominence which the charters of the Shrewsbury Gilds gave to the procession has been sufficiently pointed out already. Every care was taken to secure its fitting glory and splendour. Among the goods of the companies which the inventories name are "Baners," "Baners for ye Mynstrellys werying," "skukions for my'strells," "torches," "coots of sense," "stondarts of mayle," "other pec's of mayle," besides many swords and halberts, and the like.

The pageants of the Gilds. These various properties decked out the pageant which each Gild contributed to the common procession. It was exhibited by means of a wooden scaffold on wheels, differing probably but little in appearance from the drays or trollies which were utilised in later years. Dugdale in his *Antiquities of Warwickshire* relates that "before the suppression of the Monasteries this city[2] was very famous for the pageants that were played therein upon Corpus Christi Day; which, occasioning very great

---

[1] The festivities of the Preston Gild were held at intervals of twenty years. The last took place in 1882 (cf. Abram, *Memorials*), but many features place the Preston pageants in a different class from that to which those of Shrewsbury and Coventry belong.

[2] i.e. Coventry.

confluence of people thither from far and near, was
of no small benefit thereto : which pageants being
acted with mighty state and reverence by the friars
of this house had theaters for the several scenes,
very large and high, placed upon wheels, and drawn
to all the eminent parts of the city for the better
advantage of the spectators."

At Shrewsbury there appears never to have been
an elaborate miracle play presented by the crafts[1].
Most likely the Show early took that form which it
exhibited in the later times of which we have more
definite record. The Gilds of the town walked in
the procession, each member bearing, in mediæval
days, a light "in honour of the Blessed Sacrament,"
the officers wearing their liveries and carrying the
banners and other insignia, and thus escorting a
tableau more or less appropriate to the craft. No
small expense and even taste appears to have been
expended on these representations, though their
precise suitability it is in some cases difficult to
appreciate. Before Reformation times the tableaux
were generally of a biblical or ecclesiastical nature :
after the 16th century they were usually mytho-
logical or historical. Thus the Tailors were presided
over by Adam and Eve "the first of their craft," or by
Queen Elizabeth in ruffles of right royal magnitude.
The Shearmen or Clothworkers had a personation
of bishop Blasius, with a black mitre of wool and
doubtless also the wool-comb with which he had
been tortured at his martyrdom. The place of the

---

[1] Though there is no doubt that the Quarry was used for the
performance of plays by other actors. Cf. infra, p. 119.

saint was subsequently usurped by the king—
Edward IV., who was remembered as having especially cultivated the good offices of the wool-merchants.
The Skinners and Glovers were ruled by the king
of Morocco, whose "Cote" was an expensive item in
their accounts; they had also an elaborate mechanical
stag accompanied by huntsmen sounding bugle
blasts. The Smiths were appropriately represented
by Vulcan, or a knight in black armour "supported
by two attendants who occasionally fired off blunder-
busses." The Painters were accustomed to find
their best representative of later years in a cheery-
looking Rubens brandishing palette and brush,
while the Bricklayers, for some occult reason, considered themselves adequately represented by bluff
king Hal. The twin saints Crispin and Crispianus
patronised the Shoemakers, and S. Katharine (at
a spinning wheel) the Barbers. Venus and Ceres
presided over the Bakers.

*The Re-
formation.*   At the Reformation the Corpus Christi procession
became shorn of its splendour even before it alto-
Mary.   gether ceased under Edward VI. With Mary's
attempt to revive the old order efforts were made
to restore the Show in its pristine grandeur, though
Edward VI.'s pillaging of the Gilds had rendered the
furnishing of the lights and vestments a matter of
serious difficulty. At Shrewsbury the municipal
authorities endeavoured to keep up the mystery
plays by means of contributions from the various
companies.

Elizabeth.   The accession of Elizabeth was not likely to do
any harm to the plays and pageants, though the

outward reason for their performance might be changed. Elizabeth fully perceived the political and social usefulness of such festivities: her provincial progresses were a succession of brilliant shows and interludes which served a useful purpose in diverting the nation's attention from the graver dangers which threatened England during the queen's eventful reign. Elizabeth was also naturally fond of gaiety and wit, and the tone of the people from the highest to the lowest was dramatic. The Court had its "master of the revels," the Universities and Inns of Court had their regular plays. Interludes were provided for the queen's entertainment as she moved from town to town both at the houses of the higher gentry and by the common people. They were indeed the ordinary means by which honour was paid to any very distinguished visitor.

The Shrewsbury playwright was Thomas Ashton the first master of the grammar school. His theatre was the open ground without the walls, the Quarrell or Quarry. The season of the year at which these performances of Thomas Ashton took place was Whitsuntide, at which time Chester was also engaged in its more famous productions. It is to be regretted that no records[1] remain of these Shrewsbury plays, or a valuable addition might be made to the scanty collections of such antiquities which have been made

---

[1] Phillips (p. 201) gives the titles of two of these plays: "Julian the Apostate" (at which Elizabeth intended to be present, but was misinformed as to the date: when she arrived at Coventry tidings reached her that it was already performed) in 1565, and "The Passion of Christ" in 1567.

public. These academic entertainments did not
supplant the old annual procession (the date of
which was transferred to the Monday following the
feast of Corpus Christi) which continued apparently
until the power of the Puritans became too strong
to admit of its longer existence. Already that
influence was at work, and Elizabeth had many
detractors among those of the stricter persuasion.
The character of their sternness, as well as the
nature of their dissatisfaction at the gaiety which
Elizabeth fostered, is well exemplified at Shrewsbury
in the incident of the Shearmen's tree. The event
is also noteworthy as being the only occasion until
later days on which anything like friction occurred
between the companies and the municipal corporation[1].

The Shear-men's tree. The woollen trade, as we have seen[2], gave
occupation to a very large number of Shearmen.
These belonged to the more unskilled class of
labourers, the work they performed being simply
that of preparing the wool for the later stages of
manufacture. They were precisely the class to fail
to appreciate the religious changes, and such as
would be likely to resort to the physical force
argument on any occasion. It was also to such
men that the revelry of Christmastide, Maytime,
and the like were most precious. Their life was a
hard and colourless one, and they would for this
reason cling desperately to the old occasions of
merriment. The festival which appears to have

[1] Cf. supra, pp. 5, 36, 85, 92, 98–9.
[2] Cf. supra, p. 90.

been particularly odious to the Puritans was that
of May Day, when, Stow[1] tells us, it was the custom for the citizens " of all estates " to have their
" Mayings," and to " fetch in Maypoles, with divers
warlike shows, with good archers, morris dancers,
and other devices for pastime all the day long;
and toward the evening they had stage plays, and
bonfires in the streets." To the youth of the town
it was a sufficiently harmless summer holiday. To
the precise it was plainly and purely a heathen
survival. At Shrewsbury they were early in active
antagonism to it. In 1583 there occurred " soom
contrav'sie about the setting upp of maye poales
and bonfyers mackinge and erection of treese before
the sherman's haule and other places[2]," though
apparently without immediate effect, for two years
later appears another entry " Pd. for cutting down
the tree, and the journeymen to spend xv[d].[3]"

But it was not long before the Puritans prevailed.
The May Day merry-making was stopped and even
the Gild festival prohibited. " This yeare [1590–1]
and the 6 day of June beinge Soondaye and the
festivall day of the Co[y] of the Shearmen of Salop
aboute the setting upp of a greene tree by serte
yonge men of the saide Co[y] before their hall doore
as of many years before have been acostomid but
preachid against by the publicke precher there and
commawndid by the baylyffs that non sutche shoulde
be usid, and for the disobedience therein theye were
put in prison and a privey sessions called and there
also indicted and still remayne untill the next towne

[1] Stow's *Survey*, p. 124.   [2] Shearmen's records.   [3] *Ibid.*

sessions for further triall[1]." The letter of the law
however was in their favour. At the sessions the
judges decided that the tree should be erected
and "usyd as heretofore have be' so it be don
syvely and in lovynge order w[th]out contencion[2]."
But the soreness remained and the Shearmen were
very turbulent for a long period. A curious entry
in 1596 betokens a continuance of the friction:
"P[d] oure fyne for not rerynge of Cappes to Mr
Bayliffe 3/4[3]." For Puritan influence had waxed
stronger, and at length it was "agreed that there
shall not be hereafter any interludes or playes within
this town or liberties uppon anye Soundays or in
the night tyme. Neyther shall there be any play-
inge at footballe, or at hiltes or wastrells, or beare
baytinge, within the walles of this towne[4]."

*Common-
wealth.* During the civil wars and under the rule of the
Commonwealth the inhabitants of the town were too
heavily burdened with taxes for the maintenance of
soldiers and for the repairs of the walls (for which
the companies were severally assessed) to have much
wealth to expend on revelry and merry-making,
even had Puritan sourness admitted any such. But
*The Re-
storation.* the reaction consequent on the Restoration brought
back the glory to Shrewsbury. The agriculture of
the district had now quite recovered from the long-
distant Welsh ravages: the internal trade of the
town was also very considerable. Shrewsbury was
therefore a place of no small importance. It played
the part of a local metropolis in which the fashions

[1] Taylor MS.   [2] Shearmen's records.   [3] *Ibid.*
[4] (1594.) Owen and Blakeway, Vol. I. p. 396.

of the capital were mimicked by the wealthy trades-
folk, their wives and daughters, and the country
gentry and their families. For neither class could
often go to London. Travelling was a serious affair
not lightly to be undertaken. Consequently, just
as the country gentleman now spends a portion of
the year in London, so his ancestor in the seventeenth century made the adjacent county town his
residence at certain seasons. Besides "he was often
attracted thither by business and pleasure, by assizes,
quarter sessions, elections, musters of militia, festivals
and races...There were the markets at which the
corn, the cattle, the wool, and the hops of the surrounding country were exposed for sale...There were
the shops at which the best families of the neighbourhood bought grocery and millinery[1]." In Shrewsbury did the provincial beaux and belles promenade
by the side of the Severn and in the abbey gardens.
These latter were especially attractive. They were
laid out "with gravell walks set full of all sorts of
greens—orange and Lemmon trees...Out of this
went another garden much larger with severall fine
grass walks kept exactly cut and roled for company
to walk in: every Wednesday most of ye town y^e
Ladies and Gentlemen walk there as in St James's
Parke, and there are abundance of people of quality
lives in Shrewsbury[2]."

Farquahar in his sprightly comedy *The Recruiting Officer* describes the lively doings of the same

[1] Macaulay, *History of England*, Vol. i. p. 164.
[2] *Through England on a Side Saddle in the time of William
and Mary, being the Diary of Celia Fiennes.*

"people of quality," and also of the more stolid
burghers. "I have drawn," he says, "the Justice
and the Clown in their *Puris Naturalibus*; the one
an apprehensive, sturdy, brave blockhead; and the
other a worthy, honest, generous gentleman, hearty
in his country's cause and of as good an understanding as I could give him, which I must confess
is far short of his own." Farquahar seems to have
obtained a particularly good impression of the worthy
Salopians. He dedicates his comedy to "All Friends
round the Wrekin." "I was stranger to everything
in Salop but its Character of Loyalty, the Number
of its Inhabitants, the Alacrity of the Gentry in
Recruiting the Army, with their generous and hos-
pitable Reception of Strangers. This Character I
found so amply verify'd in every Particular that
you made Recruiting, which is the greatest Fatigue
upon Earth to other, to be the greatest Pleasure in
the World to me[1]." Shrewsbury was one of the
gayest of those many provincial capitals "out of
which the great wen of London has sucked all the
life[2]."

*Shrews-
bury Show
in 17th
century.*
Farquhar may have seen the old Show, which
the Restoration had naturally brought back, wend
its noisy way to Kingsland. The procession itself
was easily rehabilitated, but the arbours on Kingsland, where the day was spent in merrymaking,
called for much attention. Great activity was
evinced in their repair, for they had fallen into sad
decay during the hard rule of the Puritans. Some

[1] From the dedication to *The Recruiting Officer*.
[2] Thackeray, *The Four Georges*, p. 320.

of the companies adorned their arbours with gateways, arms and mottoes, "dyalls," and the like.
Most of the gateways were of wood, but in 1679
the Shoemakers company erected a handsome stone
portal, which a few years subsequently they adorned
with figures of their patron saints, Crispin and
Crispianus. As though the events of a century
previous were still fresh in men's minds, the legend
was painted underneath,

"We are but images of stonne
Do us no harme—we can do nonne."

About this time it is evident the Show was in
a very prosperous condition. Puritanism had not
taken any real hold on the country, and the Church
was restored, and old ways of thinking and acting
brought back, without any disturbance or opposition[1].
Even in the companies the religious element which
was so strong in the earlier Gilds was not entirely
wanting: the day's proceedings included a sermon in
the Church[2]. In the morning the Wardens and
members met in the open space before the castle,
whence they passed in a merry procession through
the gaily decked streets to Kingsland. There each
Gild had its arbour surrounded by trees and supplied
with tables and benches. The mayor and corporation
used to attend, and were accustomed to visit each
arbour in succession. The remainder of the day
passed in festivity and merriment, and the craftsmen
with their friends returned home in the evening

---

[1] Perry, *Church History*, Vol. ii. p. 512.

[2] Glovers' records, 1781. "Item, 1/- for carrying the Flag to
Church on Show Day."

"much invigorated with the essence of barley-corn," as a writer of fifty years ago expresses it.

Degeneracy.

But the degeneracy of the revived Show was very apparent. The dropping off of the sermons deprived the companies of the last trace of that strong religious element which had characterised their mediæval ancestors. A private letter of 1811 says, "Shrewsbury Show was on the 19th [of June] but I did not go to it. That, like other things, is getting much worse." The Drapers and Mercers had never gone to Kingsland, and gradually the other companies began to withdraw from the Show. The formal procession became confined practically to apprentices[1], while the masters contented themselves with a dinner at one of the inns of the town[2]. Everything was significant of the approaching end of the pageant.

Reform agitation tends to check degeneracy,

When the Reform agitation threatened to deprive the companies of their trading privileges at no distant period, and later, when it had succeeded in doing so, attempts seem to have been made to bring into prominence their social aspect[3], and the procession was again reinvigorated. The pomp which signalised George the Fourth's coronation may also have given a stimulus to pageantry. The arbours were repaired and rebuilt, and the year 1849 wit-

---

[1] Saddlers' records, 1810. "Treasurer to pay 2 guineas to the apprentices to go to Kingsland on Show Monday, and that they may have the use of the Cloth, Flag and Streamers belonging to the Company."

[2] Saddlers' records, 1812. "That £10 be allowed to dine the company instead of going to Kingsland."

[3] Cf. infra, p. 138.

nessed a grand revival of the procession. Attempts
in this direction were now not infrequent, but were
necessarily spasmodic. Yet the time-honoured Show
was found to be possessed of wonderful vitality.
When the Municipal Corporations Act destroyed
the exclusive privileges of trading which the com- *but Reform*
panies possessed they clung to their annual feast *Acts fatal to the*
and to the yearly procession, for which they retained *Show.*
the arbours at some expense and self-denial. Gradually however as the successive freemen died the
arbours reverted one by one to the corporation of
the town; the other Gild property, which was not
already divided, was shared among surviving members,
or fell through debt or similar causes into other
hands. Kingsland itself was to revert to the town
at the decease of the last of the members of the
companies, according to an arrangement concluded
in 1862.

Even still the old Show was hard to kill. In
spite of much that was saddening, and much degradation, the procession lingered on till some twelve
or fourteen years ago, when it died a natural death.
So another link with the past was broken, and
another spot of colour wiped away from these duller
days of uniformity and routine.

CHAPTER VIII.

THE END OF THE COMPANIES.

Failure of efforts to restrict trade. THE system of elaborate organisation by which men had regulated trade in the past had given way to an equally complete system of individualism. Confused philosophical reasoning, combined with the decay of old means of regulation, had produced this anti-social state of things. Individual competition, in uncontrolled energy, reigned supreme amid almost incredible suffering and squalor. Everything which might tend to check the progress of the devastation was looked upon with suspicion and swept swiftly out of the way. All the old restraints were wanting, and self-interest alone formed the mainspring of action. To this fetish everything was sacrificed— men's bodies and men's principles. Commercial dealings took the most questionable forms: adulteration of products went on unchecked by any qualms of honesty. The companies had long ago ceased to make any attempts in the direction of industrial regulation. The whole efforts of their members were concentrated on the vain endeavour to restrict trade to the chartered towns.

Yet even the apologist for the companies, quoted at the end of the sixth chapter, was obliged to allow that in this they had failed. The result of the action of the "oppressive oligarchies" was the "excluding or discouraging the English Subjects from Trading in our greatest and best situated towns, where the markets are[1]." Shrewsbury saw the free towns around growing up to importance and outstripping her in the race for prosperity. Birmingham, not far distant, was already famous. Another free town which rose rapidly was Manchester, where most of the new industries did not come under the Apprenticeship Act, and were consequently free and unshackled. Such formidable rivals drew away trade from the old privileged boroughs. The companies were quite unable to retain their monopolies.

But more than this. Even the measure of commercial prosperity which Shrewsbury possessed —it was not small—cannot be in any appreciable degree ascribed to the companies. A writer of 1825[2] who considers the trade of the town at that date by no means "inconsiderable[3]" attributes the fact to anything rather than the "Chartered Companies[4]." "Here are two very large linen factories, besides several manufactories for starch, soap, flannels, cotton goods, an extensive iron and brass foundry,

[1] *Britannia Languens*, p. 355.
[2] *The Stranger in Shrewsbury.*
[3] *Ibid.* p. 24.
[4] *Ibid.* On p. 28 they are described as being 16 in number. They appear to have varied considerably in number at different periods.

two ale and porter breweries, a spirit distillery, etc.[1]"
"Its fabrication of threads, linen cloths etc. etc.
stands unrivalled; whilst the more common articles
of domestic life are executed in a stile of neatness,
certainly equal, if not superior, to those of any other
place of similar size[2]." The various causes which he
looks upon as conducing to this prosperity he sets
forth with considerable detail: "its contiguity to
the Principality, the facility which it possesses for
the importation and exportation of goods, by means
of its noble river and canals, and its situation as
the capital of an extensive and populous county,
combine to give it many advantages over a variety
of places equally insular[3]." That the companies had
any hand in ministering to this prosperity, or even
served any useful purpose, seems never to have so
much as occurred to him.

Struggle against intruders   Yet they were putting their charters to the
utmost use. They used every means in their power to
hold the trade. They obtained the assistance of the
municipal officers in seeking out and expelling
intruders, even hawkers and pedlars. Actions at
law became rapidly more frequent, until at last
the life of the companies becomes one long effort
to compel intruders to take up their freedom by
paying the necessary fines. The Barbers even went
so far as to prosecute men and women-servants for
presuming to dress their masters' and mistresses'
hair.

Though these measures were unsuccessful in

[1] *The Stranger in Shrewsbury*, p. 24.
[2] *Ibid.* p. 97.   [3] *Ibid.* p. 97.

attaining their object they were not without most important results.

In the first place the companies saw their stock become rapidly impoverished, and themselves on the verge of bankruptcy. So early as 1692 the Mercers were obliged to raise £50 by means of mortgage, and in the next year they were twice forced to sell some of their property. The Grocers had, half a century previously[1], noted with sorrow how "the Stock of the Company yearly decreaseth." The Barbers so early as 1744 resolve to spend no more money at Show time "except the third part of the Weavers' Bill." The Saddlers' stock in the three per cents. has to be sold to defray the charges of actions against intruders in 1810, and about the same time the Bakers' arbour was seized " on account of sustained charges against the company in an action for supposed infringement of their rights." Even the wealthy company of the Drapers had been compelled to relinquish their annual holiday, at which open house was kept for town and neighbourhood, in 1781. *impoverishes the companies,*

But worse perhaps than this was the public odium they brought upon themselves. That this was so was acknowledged in formal meeting at the close of their public life, yet it had existed long before and grew daily stronger. *and calls down public odium on them.*

These two causes would have been alone sufficient to bring about the downfall of the companies. But there were other signs of decay in plenty. Internal *Other signs of decay.*

---

[1] In 1637.

disorder was adding to the degradation into which the once honourable associations were falling. Even in 1668 the Glovers are compelled to take into

Internal disorder. account "the disorderly manner of making wardens." So late as 1832 the Saddlers inflict a fine on their steward for attending meetings in a state of intoxi-

Accounts carelessly kept. cation. The books are much less carefully kept. The Glovers' company came to an untimely end in 1810 through maladministration and carelessness in dealing with the yearly balance sheet[1]. In 1822 so great a company as the Mercers' is found appointing a committee to search for the charter, which is ultimately found in the hands of a private individual whose magnanimity in surrendering what did not belong to him is highly praised by a formal

Trade leaves them. resolution[2]. We have seen already how trade had fallen off. In 1770 a member of the Saddlers' company paid five guineas "to be for ever excused from serving the office of Steward or Warden." Private interest alone formed the motive of action in commercial dealings. The individual knew nothing of obligations due to society.

General demoralisation. Society was indeed in a state of rottenness. Outwardly there was plentiful decorum; really there was sufficient sham with its usual concomitant, laxity of morals, in a very marked degree[3]. It

---

[1] Though a few patriotic members kept the arbours etc. in repair a few years longer.

[2] "1822. Thomas Frances Dukes made a Combrother free of all expense, for his handsome conduct in giving up the Charter." (Mercers' Records.)

[3] Cf. *The Stranger in Shrewsbury*, p. 28.

could hardly be expected that this should be otherwise in the general disregard which prevailed of
all finer instincts: questionable commercial dealings
and adulteration of products, on the one hand,
were naturally accompanied by brutality and squalor
on the other. Commercial success was the only
criterion, and as the companies could not stand
the test of this touchstone of merit they were
doomed.

The Gilds of workmen in building trades had
been seriously affected, if not destroyed, long before
by the Statute 2 and 3 Edward VI. cap. 15, which
allowed "any Freemason, roughmason, carpenter,
bricklayer, plasterer," etc. "borne in this realme or
made Denizon, to work in any of the saide Crafts in
anye cittie Boroughe or Towne Corporate...albeit the
saide p'son or p'sons...doe not inhabyte or dwell in
the cittee Borough or Towne Corporate...nor be
free of the same." But in all other trades the law
had upheld the companies, and associations strong *Efforts*
as these were in antiquity were not to be destroyed *to delay*
the end.
without a struggle. In the early years of the
nineteenth century they began to think about
internal reformation, which, had it been accom-
plished with singleness of purpose, might perhaps
have secured their further usefulness and life.
The expenses connected with the annual feasts
were regulated[1]. We have seen in the foregoing
chapter how the senior members began to withdraw

[1] The Mercers decide that their dinner shall not cost above
£25.

from the dissoluteness of the Show. The actions against intruders, which had long become chronic, were pushed on with new vigour. In the hopes apparently of deciding the question once for all the Mercers' company instituted a great suit against a Mr Hart in the year 1823 which was looked upon by all parties as a test case. Two years previously a committee had been appointed to search for the charter and other documents which might be serviceable to the company in the great struggle they were apparently then meditating. The opinion of counsel was taken, and it being favourable to the company a full meeting unanimously resolved to act upon it. The first thing to be done was to retrench the expenses. It was decided that no dinner could be held that year (1823), and the annual subscriptions to the Infirmary, the Lancaster School, and other charitable objects were suspended. The costs of the actions were to be borne by all the combrethren "rateably and in proportion agreeable to the ancient custom and usage of the Company." But several resignations and withdrawals took place, which show that there was some doubt, if not as to the exact legality, at any rate as to the expediency of the step which was being taken. But the great majority were resolved to press the matter to the issue. Actions against several intruders were consolidated, and that against Mr Hart came on for trial. Important counsel were engaged, and everything was done on both sides to discover the actual state of the law. The result was a verdict entirely in favour of the company. But the assessment of

damages at a farthing (while the expenses incurred
by the company were between six and seven hundred pounds) showed how strongly public opinion
ran in a direction contrary to the mere letter of the
law[1].

The defendants however in the present case
submitted at once, and the company soon recovered
its former financial prosperity.   Its subscriptions
were again paid after a brief interval.   But it is
noticeable that actions against intruders went on
precisely as before.   The effect of this great verdict,
which was hailed with public dinners and illumina-
tions, was absolutely *nil*.

It however stimulated the efforts of the companies in the direction of reform.   In consequence of
the action the Mercers resolved that the enrolment
of apprentices (which they confessed had been
" criminally neglected ") should be better carried out
in future, and that a *bona fide* indenture for seven
years should be required in all cases before any
claim to the freedom of the company could be
admitted.   As a tangible result a new book of
apprenticeship was commenced, which continued to
be carefully and neatly kept to the end.   Its first
entry is dated August 1, 1823, though there are
several records of earlier indentures.   Its last is July
2, 1835.   A new book for recording the petitions of
foreigners to be admitted was also provided.   These

---

[1] A similar case was tried at Ludlow in 1831 when the
Hammer-men obtained a verdict in their favour and a farthing
damages.

were comparatively few in number. They extend from July 31, 1823, to June 2, 1834.

The Municipal Corporations Act. Such was the condition of the companies when the Municipal Corporations Act[1] was passed. No detailed description of this measure, albeit it was "second in importance to the Reform Act alone[2]," is needed here. As far as the companies were concerned its provisions were simple. It took away from them wholly and entirely all their exclusive privileges of trading.

" Whereas in divers cities, towns, and boroughs a certain custom hath prevailed, and certain bye-laws have been made, that no person, not being free of a city, town, or borough, or of certain guilds, mysteries, or trading companies within the same or some or one of them, shall keep any shop or place for putting to show or sale any or certain wares or merchandize by way of retail or otherwise, or use any or certain trades, occupations, mysteries, or handicrafts for hire, gain, or sale within the same : Be it enacted that, notwithstanding any such custom or bye-law, every person in any borough may keep any shop for the sale of all lawful wares and merchandizes by wholesale or retail, and use every lawful trade, occupation, mystery, and handicraft, for hire, gain, sale or otherwise, within any borough." In these words, which might seem the echo of Magna Carta[3] through the centuries, liberty of trading was made a fact throughout England.

---

[1] 5 and 6 Will. IV. c. 76.

[2] *Constitutional History of England*, Erskine May, Vol. III. p. 285.

[3] Section 41. Omnes mercatores habeant salvum et securum

It is interesting that we have recorded for us the *End of the companies.* way in which this sweeping change was received by those most concerned. The Mercers had foreseen (July 31, 1835) that it would be advisable to drop all pending actions against foreigners until the result of the Act then before Parliament should be decided. After it had become law the company met, for the last time under the old conditions, on March 25, 1836, to consider their position and to take steps for the future. It was apparently a stormy meeting. An influential minority proposed to divide the property among the members there and then, and so have done with the company. It was however carried "That the chief rents…be not disposed of, but reserved to meet the payments to be made to the Alms people of St. Chad's Almshouses[1], and for other purposes." The fire engine, the company's weights and measures etc., were sold. The other companies acted in a similar manner. The Saddlers divided at once the funds which remained in the treasurer's hands, and which amounted to £1. 7s. 0d. for each member[2]. Their arbour was however retained, and the rent from it expended on the annual feast on Show Monday. This arrangement was to continue so long as any of the freemen should be living: on the decease of the last survivor the arbour was to devolve to the town council. Lastly,

---

exire de Anglia, et venire in Angliam, et morari et ire per Angliam, tam per terram quam per aquam, ad emendum et venendum, sine omnibus malis toltis.

[1] These were finally pulled down in 1859.

[2] The Mercers followed this example in 1878.

all books, and whatever else remained to the company, were to be deposited with the wardens for the time being.

Partial continuation of the companies. For attempts were made, even in the desperate pass to which the companies seemed to be brought, to prolong the end. A few patriotic members kept up the shadows of the old fraternities. The ancient custom of electing officers was maintained; the Mercers' records bring the lists complete down to 1876. The arbours were repaired, mostly at the cost of private individuals, and at spasmodic intervals, while the Show still continued to afford opportunities for dissolute revelry to the lowest of the town and neighbourhood. The companies themselves fell back into their original condition of voluntary associations of individuals united for purposes partly benevolent but mainly social, and of which the state took no cognisance. "No one can give much attention to the subject without coming to the conclusion that feasting was one of the essential and most valued features of the companies in their early days[1]:" it became so again in their later. As they had existed long before external circumstances brought them into prominence, so they continued long after they had ceased to influence public affairs, and so they lingered on even after the nation had plainly signified that their existence was not only superfluous but injurious. For their endeavours to restrict trade had been, so far as they had been successful, detrimental to the prosperity of the town, while they had allowed the

---

[1] *Quarterly Review*, Vol. 159, p. 50.

duty of succouring needy workmen to slip entirely
from their hands.

The Friendly Societies which had long taken up
this very important part of the functions which the
mediæval Gilds had performed rose meanwhile into
public favour. Their excellent work was so apparent
that an Act of Parliament was passed for their encouragement in 1793, and it was even urged that
they should be made compulsory.

The companies had to all intents and purposes
long forgotten their duty in this respect, and they
could not take it up again now, though had this
course been possible they might have commended
themselves to public favour. There was only one *Their*
means which kept them alive. The secret of their *property gives them*
vitality was their possession of property[1], and as that *life.*
melted away the companies were found dropping
out of existence. For being deprived of their real
essence they had nothing to recommend them. Even
the Show degenerated into a public scandal, and
the companies, like their annual pageant, at length
died, one by one, unnoticed and unregretted[2].

Yet there was arising, even at the time when the *Return to organi-*
old companies were being destroyed, a movement in *sation.*
favour of some return to organisation and regulation.

---

[1] *Quarterly Review*, Vol. 159, p. 56. The Drapers' company at
Shrewsbury still survives to manage S. Mary's Almshouses.

[2] In 1835 there appear to have been companies in at least the
following other towns in England, Alnwick, Bristol, Carlisle,
Chester, Coventry, Durham, Gateshead, Haverfordwest, Kendal,
Kingston-on-Thames, Lichfield, London, Ludlow, Morpeth, New-
castle-on-Tyne, Oxford, Preston, Richmond, Ruthin, Sheffield,
Southampton, Wells, and York.

Organisation indeed seems to have been a character-istic of the English people at all stages of their history. The Saxons had their Frith Gilds and their Monks' Gilds; the English of the Middle Ages had their Merchant, Religious, Social, and Craft Gilds; in the sixteenth century they had their Trade Societies, the direct and in many cases the little-altered suc-cessors of the Craft Gilds. Then came the larger Regulated Companies, which also had some features in common with the mediæval Gilds, more with the sixteenth century societies. The main differences between the earlier associations and those of a later date lay in the avowed motive of confederacy and in the nature of the influence they exercised. The ostensible motive of the Gilds was the general welfare: in the case of the companies it was indi-vidual gain. The influence of the Gilds may be called a healthy social and moral influence[1]; that of the post-reformation companies in the towns was in the main directed to selfish and political ends[2].

New organisations, adapted to altered conditions of life and new modes of thought, resembling and yet differing from the Gilds, were now to arise and take the place of the companies as these had taken the place of the mediæval fraternities. The growth of these however will be beyond the scope of the present essay.

It was doubtless necessary that the companies should be pulled down from the lofty heights which they once had occupied. It was requisite that all

[1] Cf. supra, pp. 47—51.
[2] Cf. supra, pp. 105—106.

relics of the detailed system of trade-organisation which the Middle Ages had handed down to us should be broken up, to make room for a *régime* more conformable to modern conditions of industry. The anarchic reign of individualism through which trade passed at the beginning of this century was an unavoidable step in economic development.

But it was a step attended with infinite loss and inestimable suffering, and it is well that proofs are not wanting of the approaching end of unrestrained competition and anti-social individualism. Signs of change are not wanting. Experience is continually demonstrating that organisation can accomplish vastly more than individual enterprise · that combination is immeasurably more powerful than competition. It is indeed the tracing out of this reaction in favour of combination for common ends, which lends to the economic history of the last hundred years its chief, perhaps its only, human interest.

The reaction has manifested itself in various *Socialists* ways. The *Socialists* have always made State-organisation of labour one of the strongest planks of their platform[1]. At the same time Englishmen have looked with peculiar jealousy on any attempts by the state to extend its sphere of action. Nevertheless a steady development has been witnessed in this direction; the various Civil Services show a uniform increase with the numbers and requirements of the nation. The Board of Trade, the Local *and other* Government Board, the Charity and Ecclesiastical *forms of organisation.*

[1] Howell, *Conflicts of Capital* etc., p. 494.

Commissioners, are further indications of the same tendency towards organisation.

The Gilds cannot, as we have seen, be censured for low aims; moreover their endeavours to reach the level they set themselves were constant and sincere. And the latter half of the nineteenth century has seen a repetition of somewhat similar attempts.

Trades Unions;

The Trades Union movement[1] is one pregnant with promise for the future[2]. Though the Unions were formed in the first instances for the purpose of resistance to the masters, it may be hoped that as the need for this grows weaker the analogy which their promoters love to institute between them and the old Craft Gilds may become more and more real. They have already done much to raise the condition of labour, and as Friendly Societies they are of the highest value to the workmen[3]. There are signs too that we may even obtain organisations which, with due allowance for altered conditions, may accomplish much of the other good work which Gilds performed for mediæval industry.

their achievements. Improvement in status of labour.

The Unions already aim at ensuring stability of employment through deliberate regulation of trade. By this means they hope to strike a death-blow at

Attempts at regulation of trade.

---

[1] The story of the rise of Trades Unions has been told with much detail by Mr G. Howell in his *Conflicts of Capital and Labour*, and by Dr Brentano in the last portion of his Essay on Gilds.

[2] It is to be hoped that the development of the "New Unionism" will not frustrate this hope.

[3] Mr John Burns has recently been urging on Trades Unions the advisability of surrendering this feature, so that the funds may the more completely be devoted to militant purposes.

that root-evil of our present industrial system, irregularity of employment and uncertainty of wages.

But they yet fall short of the Gilds in two *Further* important particulars, and until these deficiencies *necessary approxi-* are made good Trades Unions can only be considered *mation to* as insufficient means to a highly desirable end. *Gilds.*

In the first place there must be no association *Apprecia-* of men against masters, or masters against men, but *tion of the common* union of men with masters for the common good of *interests of* the craft. Fifty years ago it was pointed out[1] that *masters and men,* "the recent destruction of the old Gilds was a purely negative policy, which required to be followed up by a reconstruction on similar, but modified, lines[2]." But of course nothing was attempted, though it is for their care in seeing that the public was well served that the Gilds are chiefly praised to-day.

In the second direction much less advance has *and of the* been made[3]. Yet it cannot be expected that a high *necessity of ensuring*

[1] By Henry Lytton Bulwer, M.P., in a letter to the Handloom weavers when they petitioned for the creation of gilds of trade.

[2] Foxwell, *Irregularity of Employment*, p. 72.

[3] "There is of late a partial revival of good workmanship in many trades...but it will require years of toil to recover our lost ground in the markets of the world." G. Howell, *Conflicts of Capital* etc., p. 225. Prof. Foxwell points out that "the master cutlers of Sheffield have done something in [the] direction lately of exposing and punishing falsification" etc., *Irregularity of Employment* etc., p. 80 and note. Mr E. J. Poynter notices that "the firm of which Mr William Morris is the head, of which indeed he is the sole member, started the idea, now well understood, that the only possible means of producing work which shall be satisfactory from every side is to return to the principles on which all works of art and art-manufacture were executed, not only in the Middle Ages, but at all epochs up to the beginning of this century." *Ten Lectures on Art*, p. 274.

144   THE END OF THE COMPANIES.

a higher standard of work.

standard of wages is to be maintained unless a high standard of workmanship is also ensured. Improvement in pay can only with justice accompany improvement in skill and application. Something of the sentiment and tradition of good work which so strongly characterised the Middle Ages must be brought back. As yet it is wofully lacking. Up to the present the Trades Unions have made no real attempt to grapple with this evil, though its removal is a necessary preliminary to anything like completeness in our industrial reformation. Until they can show their ability to direct trade in this respect in a manner more beneficial to the community than competing capitalists have done during the past, the student will find their analogy to the mediæval Gilds incomplete (and that in a point where the latter might be followed with benefit), and the public will consider their usefulness to society unsatisfactory.

APPENDIX I.

NON-GILDATED TRADESMEN[1].

THE ordinary authorities on Economic history say little or nothing of the non-gildated tradesmen in the towns, though these formed an important portion of the commercial community. To understand fully the conditions under which trade was carried on in mediæval England the existence of such unfree merchants must be taken into account and their importance appreciated.

Within the commercial class the enforcement of the Gild regulations doubtless depended very largely on circumstances and individual temperament. Moreover their reiteration evidences their futility in attaining the objects they had in view. There must have been much greater freedom and elasticity of thought and action during the Middle Ages than is generally recognised.

It must be remembered too that there were important exceptions to the regulations of the Gilds. The king's servants, when exercising the royal privileges of purveyance and pre-emption, were naturally unrestricted.

---

[1] This paper was written for the Shropshire Archæological and Natural History Society, and was printed in substance in their *Transactions*, 2nd Series, Vol. III., Part ii., p. 253.

In Fair-time—and the Fairs were a very important feature in mediæval life—there was unrestrained freedom of trade. But more important than these was another. It was quite possible for ungildated tradesmen to purchase temporary or partial exemption from the local restrictions.

It will be observed that the royal charters which authorise the Gilds and grant exclusive privileges of trading differ somewhat in later years from those of the earliest date. In the earliest grants the words simply allude to the Gild only. Henry II.'s Charter to Lincoln is "Sciatis me concessisse civibus meis Lincolniæ...gildam suam mercatoriam." There is no hint of any tradesmen external to the Gild. But early in the thirteenth century it becomes evident that such stringent exclusiveness could not be enforced. The charter which Henry III. granted to Shrewsbury in 1227 confirmed the Gild in the following terms:—"Concessimus etiam eisdem Burgensibus et heredibus eorum quod habeant Gildam Mercatoriam cum Hansa et aliis consuetudinibus et libertatibus ad Gildam illam pertinentibus, et quod nullus qui non sit in Gilda illa mercandisam aliquam faciat in predicto Burgo *nisi de voluntate eorundem Burgensium.*" At about the same time the Earl of Chester and Huntingdon gave a charter to Chester forbidding trade in the town "nisi ipsi cives mei Cestrie et eorum heredes *vel per eorum gratum.*" The phrase "nisi de voluntate eorundem Burgensium (or Civium)" now became usual in the charters. In those granted by Edward I. to the towns which he founded in Wales, and which may be looked upon in some measure as model town constitutions, the provision appears in each. Thus it may be said that by the end of the thirteenth century it had become customary for the town authorities to grant exemptions from the Gild restrictions by their own authority. They practically gave over to the Gilds the supervision of trade, but at the same time retained in their own hands the power of admitting traders without obliging them to join the mercantile fraternities.

This power of granting exemptions from the restrictions of the Gilds seems to have been exercised in various towns in different degrees. In some it extended no further than the permitting "foreigners" to come to casual markets on payment of a toll upon each occasion. In others however it was more largely and generally used, merchants being allowed to be resident and to trade continually and regularly by payment of an annual fine.

In the latter case the effect was to create two distinct classes of traders within the town. The burgesses may be divided into two classes, those of them who were gildsmen and those who were not. We now see that the tradesmen dwelling in the towns may similarly be divided into two classes, (i) those who were free of the town or of one of the Gilds (or free both of the town and one of its Gilds), and (ii) those who were neither burgesses nor gildsmen. Thus another has been added to the classes into which the inhabitants of towns are usually divided. Mention of these *unfree* tradesmen is found in the records of many towns in England and Wales : in Norwich, Winchester, Lincoln, Leicester, Andover, Yarmouth, Canterbury, Henley-on-Thames, Malmesbury, Bury S. Edmunds, Totnes, Wigan, Chester, Shrewsbury, Worcester, Clun, Brecknock, Neath, Bishops' Castle, and others.

The designation of these unfree tradesmen varies. At Andover they were known as *custumarii* (in opposition to the *hansarii*—the full members of the Gild).

At Canterbury a similar body appears under the name of *intrants*. In Scotland and the north of England they were called *stallingers*. The most usual name for them is however *censer, chencer, tenser*, and variations of these.

Censer is apparently the name applied to one who pays a *cense* or *cess*. In Domesday mention is made of *censarius*—"Ibi sunt nunc 14 censarii habentes septem carucatas"—and the *censarius* is described as "qui terram ad censum annuum tenet." The connection of the word is here purely territorial. It becomes more personal later in the history as is seen in the "Compotus Civitatis Wyntoniæ" of the third year of Edward I., which contains the following entry :—"Et de xliiijs. ijd. ob. de hominibus habitacionibus in civitate Wynton' qui non sunt de libertate, qui dicuntur Censarii, per idem tempus." Here the *censarii* are evidently considered in their capacity not as possible landowners, but solely as tradesmen. The *census* has changed from the land rent of Domesday to a distinctly personal payment.

A somewhat different class from the *censarii* of Winchester are mentioned in the statute 27 Henry VIII., cap. 7. From the preamble we can form a good idea of the lawlessness and confusion which prevailed on the borders of Wales at that period. It is related that in the Marches, where thick forests frequently fringe the roads, "certain unreasonable Customs and Exactions have been of long time unlawfully exacted and used, contrary both to the law of God and man, to the express wrong and great impoverishment of divers of the king's true subjects." The most crying of these evils was that the foresters were accustomed to plunder all passing along the roads (probably under the plea of taking toll), unless they bore "a Token delivered to them by the chief Foresters...or else were yearly Tributors or Chensers." The statute offers no explanation of these terms, but it is most likely they applied to persons paying an annual sum, either to the king or the Lords Marchers, of the nature of Chief Rent, especially as Cowell, in giving his explanation of the word *chenser* which will be noticed later, refers to this Act of Henry VIII. in support of his definition. If this be so we see that although the signification of the term had been extended so as to include distinctly personal and commercial tolls, it had, in some districts, also retained its original connection with land. This, censor, censer, gensor, chencer, and other variations, is the most usual form of the word, but occasionally it is found as tenser, tensor, tensur, and tensure. Tenser and tensor are used at Shrewsbury; at Worcester the same word appears as tensure or tensar (*English Gilds*, pp. 382, 394).

It is difficult to say whether or no *tenser* is a confusion of *censer*. Etymologically the words seem akin, *cense* being a tax or toll (cess), and *tensare* meaning to lay under toll or tribute. In the Iter of 1164 enquiry is directed to be made " de prisis et tenseriis omnium ballivorum domini regis...et quare prisæ illæ captæ fuerint, et per quem " etc. Another derivation of *tenser* has been given. Owen and Blakeway (Vol. ii. p. 525) explain it to be a corruption of "tenancier," and apparently intend to imply that these non-gildated traders were considered as holding directly of the king. This view receives some confirmation from Cowell's definition of the "censure" and "censers" of Cornwall. He says (*A Law Dictionary: or the Interpreter* etc., ed. 1727) "**Censure**, or *Custuma vocata* **censure**, (from the Latin *Census*, which Hesychius expounds to be a kind of personal money, paid for every Poll) is, in divers Manors

in *Cornwall* and *Devon*, the calling of all Resiants
therein above the age of sixteen, to swear Fealty to
the Lord, to pay ij^d per *Poll*, and j^d per an. ever after ;
as *cert-money* or *Common Fine ;* and these thus sworn,
are called *Censers.*" "Chensers," he says again, "are
such as pay Tribute or *cense*, Chief-rent or Quit-rent, for
so the French *censier* signifies." Whether or no we
receive Owen and Blakeway's derivation of the word
from *tenancier*, even with the support of Cowell's
"censers" of Cornwall, we may press the latter authority into service in showing that the signification of
censer and *tenser*, however different the two words
might be in origin, became very similar in actual use.

The fines which the tensers or censers paid were
imposed in the Court Leet. On the Court Leet Rolls at
Shrewsbury are entered lists of names and fines headed
"Nomina eorum qui merchandizant infra villam Salopie
et Suburbia eiusdem, et non Burgenses, ergo sunt in
misericordia." In the first year of the reign of Henry IV.
(A.D. 1399) it was ordered that these fines should be
levied before the feast of S. Katharine (November 25) in
each year. The Court Leet also decided the amount
of the fines, but in later times when the select body of
magnates had deprived the popular courts of so many
of their powers and privileges we find that the appor-
tioning of the tensers' fines had also passed to the close
corporation. In 1519 the corporation fixed the tolls
at 6*d.* quarterly. The statute 35 Henry VIII., cap. 18,
gave the control of the unfree tradesmen in Canterbury
to the Mayor and Aldermen of the City. "No foreigner,
not being free of the said City, shall buy or sell any
Merchandize (saving Victual) to another foreigner ; nor
shall keep any shop nor use any mystery within the said
City or the liberties thereof, without the License of the

Mayor and Aldermen, or the major part of them, in writing under their Seal." At Winchester in 1650 the rates were revised by the Mayor and Aldermen. The highest limit was fixed at £5, but the fees actually paid were generally sums varying from 6*d*. to 3/4 only (Gross, II. 264).

When such a privilege was exercised by a select body it was certain to give rise to abuses. Such was found to be the case in early years when the fines were imposed by an authority other than the general assembly of burgesses. In the county court held at Lincoln in 1272 it was alleged that the late Mayor had taken pledges from the burgesses of Grimsby unjustly under the plea of exacting *gildwite* (as the fine or toll was sometimes called). We learn that at Shrewsbury in 1449–50 "this yeare the Burgesses and Tenssaars... did varye." What the cause of contention was, or how the dispute was settled, we do not know, but it could hardly arise over anything other than the question concerning the tolls to be paid by the tensers.

In some towns special civic officials were appointed to supervise the tensers. At Chester the "leave-lookers" were among the most important of the borough officers. The word *leve* or *leave* has very much the same signification as the word *cense* or cess. It is the English "levy," and was the fee or toll for permission to trade. The "leve-lookers" were the officials who exacted the levy or toll which unfree tradesmen were obliged to pay. At Chester they were "appointed annually by the Mayor for the purpose of collecting the duty of 2*s*. 6*d*. claimed by the corporation to be levied yearly upon all non-freemen who exercise any trade within the liberties of the City." Their duties are described as having been "to give Licence and compound with any that came either to

buy or sell within these liberties contrary to our grants;"
"if any did dwell within the city that were not free,
if they did ever buy or sell within the liberties, they
did likewise compound with the *Custos* and *Mercator*
[Custos Gilde Mercatorie] by the year...the Leave-
lookers do gather two pence halfpenny upon the pound,
of all Wares sold by Forraigners within the City."
(Gross, II. 42.) The same name is found at Wigan,
where the duty of the "gate-waiters or leave-lookers"
was to see that all "foreigners" paid their fines for
licence to reside and trade in the town. (Sinclair,
Wigan, passim.)

It is not easy to define the exact status of the
tensers. They were certainly considered as an inferior
body of burgesses, and might comprise three classes.
Firstly, those not willing or not able to enter one of
the gilds; secondly, traders waiting to be admitted
burgesses; thirdly ex-burgesses fallen from the higher
state through misfortune.

1. As an inferior class of tradesmen they could
only purchase their stock from townsmen (Gross, II.
177); they were incapable of bearing municipal office
(Ibid. II. 190) and they were liable to be called upon
"to be contributorie to alle the comone charges of the
Citie, whan it falleth" (*Ibid.* II. 190). In the general
course of trade but little difference might be perceptible
between the tensers and the Gildsmen, but attempts
to fuse or to confuse the two classes were jealously
resented whenever they were discovered. Naturally
these attempts to minimise the distinctions between
Gildsmen and non-gildsmen were generally prompted,
in later times, by political reasons. Only freemen of
the town and members of the companies had the privilege
of voting in Parliamentary elections, and great was the

desire to obtain a position on the list of voters. In
"An Account of the Poll for Members of Parliament
for the Borough of Shrewsbury taken June 29 and 30,
1747" etc., information is supplied concerning certain
townsmen who had claimed to be freemen but were
rejected on account of having proved themselves to be
otherwise by payment, in times past, of the tensers' fines.
Of John Bromhall, baker, we read "It was objected to
his vote that he was no Burgess, in support of which it
was proved that he had paid Tensership several years,
and that his ffather had paid toll. This Tensership is a
ffine or acknowledgement commonly paid by persons
following trade in the town that are no Burgesses, but it
being insisted that it was paid through ignorance or
mistake, his ffather was called and admitted to prove
that he had voted at a former election for this Borough,
whereupon the Mayor admitted his vote, but upon
examining a copy of the Poll for the year 1676 it
appears that all the ffamily of this Bromhall were upon
a scrutiny rejected as not Burgesses."

2. They comprised also among their number many
tradesmen waiting to be made burgesses. We learn
this distinctly from an ordinance of the corporation of
Leicester passed in the year 1467, to the effect that
every person opening a shop in the town should pay
yearly 3/4 *till he enter into the Chapman Gild.* (Nichols,
County of Leicester, I. 376.) There were several causes
which would account for the existence of this class.
The towns grew increasingly jealous of extending their
privileges, as these became valuable. The Gildsmen
would also desire to learn somewhat of the character of
the new-comer before admitting him to full membership
with themselves; while on the other hand the latter
would wish to see whether the trade of the town were

sufficiently prosperous to warrant him settling in the
borough permanently. This cause would specially ope-
rate in the case of the Welsh boroughs which grew up
after Edward I.'s conquest of the principality.

The townsmen however did not approve of the growth
of a wealthy class of traders, sharing almost equal commercial privileges with themselves and at the same time
not liable to the burdens which were the necessary
accompaniment of those privileges. They therefore
made it incumbent upon every tenser who evidently
was sufficiently satisfied with the trade of the town to
make the borough his permanent home, and who had
attained to a fair competency, that he should throw in
his lot fully and completely with them. He must become in fact a full burgess. This is carefully explained
in the *Ordinances of the City of Worcester*—regulations
concerning the trade of the town dating from the
reign of Edward IV. No. XLVII. says "Also, that euery
Tensure be sett a resonable fyne, aft^r the discression
of the Aldermen, and that euery tensure that hath ben
w^{t}yn the cyte a yere or more dwellynge, and hath
sufficiaunt to the valo^r of XLs. or more, be warned to be
made citezen, by resonable tyme to hym lymitted, and
iff he refuse that, that he shalle yerly pay to the comyn
cofre XLd., ouer that summe that he shalle yerly pay
to the Baillies or any other officers; and so yerly to
contynue tylle he be made citezen" (*English Gilds*, p.
394).

3. There were, thirdly, those who had fallen from
a higher state through misfortune or other cause. We
read of individuals surrendering their freedom and paying the tenser's fine. "He withdrew and surrendered
the freedom to the Commonalty, and now pays toll"
(Gross, II. 240).

As regarded their dealings other than commercial in nature the tendency was to assimilate the tensers and the townsmen. In a grant made to Shrewsbury by Henry VI. and confirmed by Parliament in 1445 the same privileges are extended to the tensers as are possessed by the burgesses in the matter of exemption from the necessity of finding bail in certain cases. Similarly at Worcester the "tensures" shared with the citizens the right to the assistance of the afferors in cases of wrongful or excessive amercement. (*English Gilds*, 394.)

Nevertheless where commercial privileges were at stake the distinction was rigidly preserved by every means in the possession of the townsmen. The tenser's fine was maintained up to the present century, though not without considerable difficulty. On every hand there were evidences that the companies had outlived their usefulness. Friction was everywhere injuring the social machine. Competition and individualism had taken the place of custom and co-operation. At Winchester there were grievous complaints of intruders who did "use Arts, Trades, Misteries and manual occupations...without making any agreement or composition for soe doing, contrary to the said antient usage and custome, tending to the utter undoing of the freemen... and decay of the same City." Everywhere the records of the companies detail little else than summonses to intruders to take up their freedom and notices of actions at law against them for refusing to do so. General demoralisation prevailed, and the existence of a class holding such an equivocal position as that of the unfree tradesmen did not help to mend matters. The case of John Bromhall which has been mentioned above illustrates the general looseness which prevailed in all departments of municipal administration. A ludicrous incident which happened at Shrewsbury in connection with the tensers in later years is recorded by Gough in his *Antiquities of Myddle*, published in 1834. "This Richard Muckleston was of a bold and daring spirit, and could not brook an injury offered to him. He commenced a suit against the town of Shrewsbury for exacting an imposition on him which they call tentorshipp, and did endeavor to make void their charter, but they gave him his burgess-ship to be quiet."

The companies were preserved from repetitions of this strange indignity by the passing of the Municipal Corporations Act of 1835, in consequence of which there could no longer be any invidious distinction between freemen and non-freemen, hansarii and custumarii, gildsmen and tensers.

APPENDIX II.

AUTHORITIES CITED.

Abram, W. A.—Memorials of the Preston Guilds.

An Account of the Poll for Members of Parliament for the Borough of Shrewsbury etc. (1747).

Boeckh, A.—Public Economy of Athens, translated by George Cornewall Lewis (1842).

Brentano, Lujo—On the history and development of Gilds and Origin of Trade-Unions.

"Britannia Languens, or a discourse of trade." (1680.)

Bryce, J.—The Holy Roman Empire (1887).

Cowell—A Law Dictionary: or the Interpreter etc. (1727).

Cunningham, W.—The Growth of English Industry and Commerce (1885).

Dugdale, W.—Antiquities of Warwickshire.

Ebner, Dr Adalbert—Die klösterlichen Gebets-Verbrüderungen bis zum Ausgange des Karolingischen Zeitalters (1891).

Eden, Sir F. M.—The State of the Poor.

Eyton, W.—Antiquities of Shropshire.

Farquhar—The Recruiting Officer.

Foucart—Les Associations réligieuses chez les Grecs.

Foxwell, H. S.—Irregularity of Employment and Fluctuations of Prices (1886).

Froude, J. A.—History of England from the fall of Wolsey to the death of Elizabeth (12 vols., 1862–70).

Gneist—Geschichte des Self-Government in England.

„   Das heutige Englische Verfassungs- und Verwaltungsrecht.

Gough—The Antiquities of Myddle (1834).

Green, J. R.—A Short History of the English People (1886).

Gross, Charles—The Gild Merchant (1891).

Grote, George—History of Greece (1888).

Hallam, H.—View of Europe during the Middle Ages. 1 vol.

Harrison, W.—A description of England (in "Elizabethan England," Camelot Series).

Hatch, E.—The Organisation of the Early Christian Churches (Bampton Lectures, 1881).

Howell, G.—Conflicts of Capital and Labour (1890).

Howell, Thomas—The Stranger in Shrewsbury (1825).

Kemble, J. M.—The Saxons in England.

Longfellow—The Golden Legend.

Macaulay, Lord—History of England from the Accession of James II. (1889).

May, Erskine—Constitutional History of England. 3 vols. (1887).

Merewether and Stephens—History of the Boroughs.

Nichols, J.—The History and Antiquities of the County of Leicester (1795–1815).

Ordericus Vitalis—Ecclesiastical History of England and Normandy (Bohn's Series).

Owen and Blakeway—History of Shrewsbury.

[Owen, Hugh]—Some Account of the Ancient and Present State of Shrewsbury (1808).

Perry, C. G.—A History of the English Church (Vol. II.) (1878).

Pidgeon's Memorials of Shrewsbury (old Ed.).

„ Some Account of the Ancient Gilds, Trading Companies, and the origin of Shrewsbury Show (1862).

Poynter, E. J.—Ten Lectures on Art (1880).

Quarterly Review, Vol. 159.

Riley, H. T.—Memorials of London...in the XIII, XIV, and XV Centuries.

Rogers, Thorold—Six Centuries of Work and Wages (1889).

„ The Economic Interpretation of History (1888).

Scott, Sir Walter—Marmion.

Sinclair, D.—The History of Wigan.

Smith, Toulmin—English Gilds (E. E. T. S.).

State Papers, Domestic (Elizabeth).

Statutes at Large (6 vols, 1758).

Stow, John—A Survey of London (Carisbrooke Library).

Strype—Ecclesiastical Memorials (1821).

Stubbs, W.—Constitutional History of England (1883).

„ Select Charters (1884).

„ Lectures on Mediæval History.

Taylor MS. in Library of Shrewsbury School (Reprinted in S. A. S. Vol. III.).

Thackeray, W. M.—The Four Georges.

Through England on a Side Saddle in the Time of William and Mary, being the Diary of Celia Fiennes.

Transactions of the Shropshire Archæological Society (cited as S. A. S.), Vols. I—XI.

Wordsworth, W.—The Happy Warrior.

INDEX.